T0293903

VW TYPE 2 TRANSPORTER

1949–1967

RICHARD COPPING

AMBERLEY

First published 2020

Amberley Publishing
The Hill, Stroud,
Gloucestershire, GL5 4EP

www.amberley-books.com

Copyright © Richard Copping, 2020

The right of Richard Copping to be identified as the Author
 of this work has been asserted in accordance with the
Copyrights, Designs and Patents Act 1988.

All rights reserved. No part of this book may be reprinted
or reproduced or utilised in any form or by any electronic,
mechanical or other means, now known or hereafter invented,
including photocopying and recording, or in any information
storage or retrieval system, without the permission in writing
from the Publishers.

ISBN 978 1 4456 9346 0 (print)
ISBN 978 1 4456 9347 7 (ebook)

British Library Cataloguing in Publication Data.
A catalogue record for this book is available from the British Library.

Typeset in 10pt on 13pt Celeste.
Typesetting by Aura Technology and Software Services, India.
Printed in the UK.

Contents

From Concept to Prototypes and Production

A Necessary Preamble

The vast majority of Volkswagen enthusiasts will say, if asked, that the VW Transporter, colloquially often referred to as the Campervan, was the brainchild of the entrepreneurial Dutchman Ben Pon. For their part, Volkswagen appear happy to perpetuate the legend, citing the sketch of a box-like van Pon made in April 1947 when calculating production anniversaries.

A delve into Volkswagen's tainted early history, its very existence being entirely due to the Nazi party (who funded the building of the Wolfsburg factory when established German manufacturers produced a catalogue of obstacles to building the Beetle on behalf of the state) and Hitler (who ruthlessly squashed all opposition to his plan for a motorised Germany and a people's car for the masses), reveals little or no reference to a van or commercial vehicle. Ferdinand Porsche created the car we know today as the Beetle and, as war engulfed the nation, added military variations to the theme, namely the robust all-terrain Kübelwagen and the amphibious Schwimmwagen. Meaningful development of the civilian Beetle, or KdF-Wagen (Strength-through-Joy car) as Hitler decreed it should be named, which in 1939 had not yet entered series production had ground to a halt.

The vast KdF factory was liberated by the Americans as the Allies drove ever closer to Hitler's annihilation, but its location placed it within the British zone of control. A young REME Major, Ivan Hirst, was sent to the badly bomb-damaged plant with no specific orders other than to take control. Thanks to his ad-hoc ingenuity in the face of shortages, the de-Nazification processes and the fact that nobody wanted the now ownerless factory, the Beetle was reborn, its initial purpose being to provide much needed transport for the occupying forces.

An invitation to visit Ivan Hirst at his home in a West Yorkshire village, ostensibly to discuss the Beetle and nothing more, proved invaluable when considering progress and the general atmosphere at Wolfsburg in the latter years of the 1940s. As Beetle production faltered, and it became clear that the overall aim of the British was not to remain in Germany infinitum, it was determined that the Volkswagen plant needed the support and expertise of an automobile professional. The man, chosen initially by Hirst and subsequently approved by Colonel Charles Radclyffe, head of the Military Government's light mechanical industry division at Minden, was one Heinz Nordhoff, a former Opel director. A workaholic, Nordhoff had a proven track record and was thoroughly versed in the modern production methods employed by General Motors and their rivals in Detroit. Nordhoff took up his appointment on 2 January 1948, four days before his forty-ninth birthday, not as a deputy to Hirst or anyone else, but as the recognised head of a future independent Volkswagen. From the start he made it clear that he was in charge, quickly dispensing with the services of Hermann Munch, the plant's German custodian, and consciously and effectively side-lining the amateur Hirst.

Persistent rumours have it that Hirst coveted the top job at Wolfsburg on a long-term basis, something he neither denied nor conceded when we met. What was clear, however, was the still present bitterness that existed in his feelings towards Nordhoff, the man who without Hirst's assistance, or even his presence, would create out of the Beetle the single most-produced model of all time. Nordhoff was set to revolutionise working practises at the still heavily bomb-damaged, leaking factory, where its demoralised workforce took many, many hours to build a single car. He put in place the necessary measures to ensure substantial year-by-year increases in production until the point was reached when Volkswagen could legitimately claim to be the third or fourth largest car manufacturer in the world after Ford, General Motors and, on occasion, Chrysler.

At his most outspoken, Hirst's resentment of Nordhoff and his success was blatantly obvious:

> I think you could have put anybody in there, even a monkey and it would have been a success. There was a huge factory, a labour force, a building, a good management already in place, a car that would sell, huge demand all over the world for light cars and it could not fail even if you put the biggest fool you could find in charge, it would still have worked.

On an occasion when Hirst felt more forgiving, he described his relationship with Nordhoff as 'close, but cold', but was soon to summarise the new man's attitude as being one of a 'distant figure to everybody...'

For his part, as success led to a showering of accolades, Nordhoff became equally scathing of Hirst's performance, lamenting on the task before him when he arrived at Wolfsburg. By 1954 he felt confident enough to state that:

> I was faced with a desolate heap of rubble, a horde of desperate people, the torso of a deserted town; an amorphous mass which had never had any organising principle, no factory or organisation in a real sense, without a programme or any rational work organisation. So something new had to be created because there was nothing there and had never been anything to build on at all.

The animosity between Hirst and Nordhoff has been variously presented. In the Director General's lifetime, supported by the tangible evidence of production success and ever-expanding satellites and markets and carefully nurtured by his press and public relations department, Nordhoff undoubtedly had the upper hand.

However, with Nordhoff's death at the age of sixty-nine in April 1968, while he was still in office, matters changed. During the latter months of 1966 and into 1967, West Germany experienced its first post-war recession. Concerned for his workforce and the very real prospect of having to lay men off, Nordhoff had spoken out criticising the new coalition government's policy, which he believed adversely affected the automobile industry. Predictably, the politicians rounded on him, criticising VW for relying on one model for too long, for having been asleep and hoarding considerable financial reserves. Finance Minister Franz-Josef Strauss was particularly vocal in condemning Nordhoff's lack of attention to the market, while decrying the Beetle as outdated and uncomfortable. Crucially though, as Nordhoff was past the traditional retirement age, those same politicians put in place measures to find a successor to the Director General for the largely state-owned firm, someone who would toe the line and inevitably produce new models.

While Nordhoff recognised that he couldn't delay retirement forever, his choice for a potential successor was spurned, the role of deputy being given to one Kurt Lotz by the newly appointed chairman of the supervisory board, Dr Josef Rust, a one-time aide to none other than Franz-Josef Strauss. When Lotz joined Volkswagen on 1 June 1967, Nordhoff was far from well and absent from his desk. Although he would later rally, a diagnosis of progressive heart failure spelt the end. Determined as always to prove his indestructability, the Director General finally overexerted himself once too often and died in hospital on Good Friday, 12 April 1968.

Sadly, with a background unrelated to the motor industry, Lotz floundered, his legacy, following the decision not to renew his contract in 1971, proving to be little more than a bought in and suspect water-cooled car, the K70. There was no successor to the Beetle in the pipeline. Perhaps inevitably, Nordhoff's image was tarnished too as Lotz's team consistently blamed the organisation's woes on past leadership decisions. Many of Nordhoff's achievements were simply swept under the carpet, or at least downgraded, his pivotal role in the Transporter's birth and diversity of models being a prime example.

Ben Pon Seizes an Opportunity

Predictably, any conversation with Major Ivan Hirst would be dominated by talk of the Beetle. Nevertheless, his tale of the birth of the VW Transporter, a name only allocated to the second post-war Volkswagen long after Hirst had left Wolfsburg, proved such a ripping yarn that it couldn't be excluded from his repertoire.

A notable raconteur with a natural theatrical style, complete with pregnant pauses before delivery of a punch line, the eighty-year-old-plus Hirst's starting point was the placing of an unused serviette in front of him and the retrieval of a stubby pencil from his rather baggy and battered cardigan pocket. Then he spoke of the so-called Plattenwagen, literally a flatbed 'truck', with its cab over the rear driving wheels, the chassis frame and other bits and bobs wrenched from a passing Beetle, which for reasons irrelevant to the current story was littered with parts taken from the wartime Porsche-created, Jeep-type vehicle, christened the Kübelwagen (Bucket Car). The Plattenwagen was a vehicle of Hirst's invention, his ingenious solution to the dilemma of manoeuvring parts in a vast factory and the military wanting back the equivalent of the forklift trucks they had leant to the Major.

Enter, figuratively at this stage, Ben Pon, super-salesman and joint owner of Pon's Automobeilhandel based in Amersfoort, in Holland. For a number of years, the Nazi period included, Pon had wanted to get his hands on the Beetle and, indeed, he was destined to become the first of many to arrange export of the car to lands other than

Entrepreneur Dutchman Ben Pon (pictured left with his brother, Wijnand) is often credited as the creator of the Transporter Delivery Van.

that of its native soil. Visiting the war-torn Wolfsburg factory, he spotted the Plattenwagen and immediately saw an opportunity to provide Dutch companies with an upgrade on their three-wheel delivery vans. Sadly, Pon was thwarted in his plan to line his pockets with cash, as the Dutch Transport Authority decreed that to be fully in control of a vehicle, the driver had to be seated at its front – an alien notion as far as Hirst's concept went.

Pon, of course, quickly bounced back. During his next memorable visit to Wolfsburg, on 23 April 1947, he elaborated on his Plattenwagen inspired 'design' by sketching its outline in the notebook he carried with him wherever he went. This takes the tale back to Ivan Hirst, who with his pencil carefully poised over his improvised serviette sketchpad now meticulously replicated Pon's thankfully preserved 'artwork'. As his drawing emerged, and with a remarkably steady hand for an old and physically frail man, Ivan explained the Pon concept. The structure was box-like, with its engine over the rear axle and the cab over the front wheels, creating a stable home for an alleged 750 kg of goods, bulky, heavy or otherwise.

The sketch completed, Ivan was keen to move towards other topics, leaving in the trail of the story the implication that mass production of the 'new' Delivery Van followed. In fairness to the former REME Major, Volkswagen too cites the birth of the Transporter as that celebrated sketch. Unfortunately, life was not that simple, however much (for varying reasons) both Pon and Hirst might have wished it. Hirst couldn't make such a significant move without consulting his boss, Colonel Charles Radclyffe. Frankly, the Colonel wasn't interested; more burning issues determined his cursory decision. He deemed Hirst's main priority to be failing Beetle production. The order books were full, but month-on-month

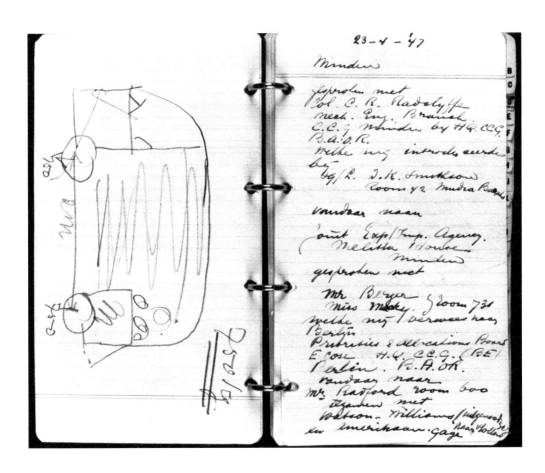

Above: Ben Pon's famous sketch of a delivery vehicle – hastily scribbled in his notebook during his visit to Wolfsburg and Major Ivan Hirst on 23 April 1947.

Left: Major Ivan Hirst – the British Officer in charge at Wolfsburg in the immediate post-war years.

production was slipping away. The factory was still, in parts, ruinous. Building Beetles under tarpaulins was not uncommon and the lack of available labour was a very real concern. With such a mass of dark clouds hovering, considering a second Volkswagen, however attractive the van concept might be, was crazy. How Radclyffe conveyed such a message to Hirst is unclear, but without any shadow of doubt the go-ahead was refused in all shapes and forms.

Seeing this latest potential moneymaking venture evaporate before his eyes, Pon shrugged his broad shoulders, figuratively tore up his sketch and concentrated on other things, most notably taking delivery of his first six Beetles on 8 August 1947. Meanwhile, Radclyffe, aware that Volkswagen's longer-term future didn't lie with the British and no doubt conscious that Hirst was a gifted amateur rather than a car man through and through, charged the Major with finding a pair of capable German hands to drive the business forward. Ivan Hirst unearthed Heinz Nordhoff, who at the time was managing the service department of an Opel garage on behalf of the widow of a pre-war dealer.

From Rags to Riches with Dr Nordhoff

Colonel Radclyffe's appointment of ex-Opel director Heinz Nordhoff as Director General of Volkswagen was an astute move. Nordhoff quickly identified the problems afflicting Volkswagen. He variously described the Beetle, Wolfsburg's only model at the time of his arrival, as being 'still full of bugs', possessed of 'more flaws than a dog has fleas', 'a small cheap thing' and 'an ugly duckling'.

> There was so much to be done. Weak points in the design had to be ironed out, bottlenecks in production had to be broken, and problems of material procurement, quality control, personnel had to be solved.

However, the ultimate dilemma was that 'seven thousand workers were painfully producing six thousand cars a year, provided it did not rain too much. Most of the roof and all of the windows had been destroyed...'

Nordhoff's strategy was to produce a Beetle people wanted, not just in Germany but also across Europe and beyond: a reliable car painted and trimmed to a standard sufficient to call it a De Luxe limousine; a vehicle capable of raising cash to invest in refurbishment, presses and other equipment. Anything not central to this goal, the key example being production of the niche market soft-top version of the Beetle, was simply farmed out, coachbuilders Karmann of Osnabrück being eager to oblige.

Production escalated to such an extent that by 1955, the millionth Beetle had been built, while, even at the start of the 1960s, Volkswagen's inability to produce sufficient cars, no matter how much more money was invested in the tools of ever greater production, resulted in supply still falling short of demand. In 1965, Volkswagen produced in excess of one million Beetles within a twelve-month period.

Alongside the De Luxe or Export model Beetle, Nordhoff saw an urgent need for one other Volkswagen. Its purpose was diverse. The Beetle was unsuitable for adaption into a delivery vehicle – a van. Similarly, despite attempts to depict it as a family saloon with five occupants, the Beetle was a small car. Larger, growing families and many businesses needed a new concept in motoring – a people carrier. If possible, as money was tight, the new vehicle should share many components with the Beetle. Whether Pon's sketch for a Delivery Van was used as a reference point is unclear, what is though is that Nordhoff's concept was far wider in vision and altogether more embracing.

Volkswagen's MD Calls a Press Conference

Sadly, the death of Heinz Nordhoff while he was still in office deprived budding authors of the cosy retirement *tête-à-têtes* enjoyed by those of us who met Ivan Hirst. Fortunately, Nordhoff's set-piece words survive, as apart from a reasonable supply of newspaper and magazine interviews, the pre-delivery texts of his many speeches are carefully filed away in the VW archive, itself located in what was once the dining room of Volkswagen's bigwigs, Nordhoff included. It was to these that my access was kindly afforded by VW, the nearest any author today can possibly achieve to meeting the great man. No doubt as an aid to perfect delivery, each speech was double-space-typed by some long-suffering, but undoubtedly admiring, secretary, while most are annotated with last-minute pencil amendments made in Nordhoff's own neat and readily legible hand.

Inevitably, a primary aim of delving into the VW archives was to soak up the words delivered by Nordhoff at the press launch of the VW Transporter, a more intimate style of address nevertheless given to a crowded room of eagerly inquisitive journalists on a cold November's day in 1949. The text was lengthy, although there is nothing unusual in that where Nordhoff was concerned and whilst not openly repetitive, it was clearly composed to emphasise the key selling points of the new Volkswagen. While not a huge amount was said concerning the variety of Transporters planned, the pictorial evidence of the presence of not just two prototype Delivery Vans, but also what was referred to as the 'Kombi' and a more up-market passenger-carrying vehicle, was sufficient to confirm model diversity from the earliest days.

Nordhoff began by advising his eager audience that 'this vehicle was planned just over a year ago during a car journey I made with Dr Haesner'. No mention was made of Hirst, who had left Wolfsburg for the last time just three months previously, or for that matter Ben Pon, despite his larger-than-life presence in the audience. Fresh from the launch of a revitalised and now readily saleable Beetle, Nordhoff clearly wished to dissociate himself from any form of British intervention in the development of the new model and if that severed the link with Pon by default, so be it. As for the reference to Alfred Haesner, he'd been appointed in 1948 as Head of Technical Development and was set to remain with Volkswagen until 1952. From there, he joined Ford in Germany, where his main claim to fame was the creation of the first Transit van. The Transporter was Haesner's creation but only under Nordhoff's micro-management.

As a result of market research involving hundreds of individual interviews, Nordhoff advised his audience it was clear 'that it was not the typical half-tonne on a car chassis that was required, but a fifty per cent bigger three-quarter-tonner with as large as possible load space; an enclosed vehicle which can be used in many different ways'.

Determined to divulge the secret recipe for the VW Transporter's potential success, Nordhoff elaborated on the ingredients of the thought process:

Heinz Nordhoff – Director General of Volkswagen AG 1948–1968 and the man who brought his concept of a multi-purpose vehicle into reality.

We didn't begin from the basis of an existing chassis, as this would have badly hindered the logical solution we wanted, but instead we started from the load area – actually much more obvious and original. The Transporter comprises a main area of three-square metres of floor space plus, over the engine, an additional square metre and forty-five cubic metres of volume ... All this is produced as a complete self-supporting steel superstructure, with a low and unobstructed loading area ... This vehicle weighs 875kg in road-going condition and carries 850kg, thus representing a best-ever performance for a van of this size, with a weight to load ratio of 1:1 ... With this vehicle, the load area lies exactly between the axles. The driver at the front and the engine at the rear, match each other extremely well in terms of weight. The axle load is always equal, whether the vehicle is empty or laden.

After offering greater levels of detail in respect of every possible innovation, Nordhoff's conclusion was suitably rousing:

With our new Volkswagen we have created a new vehicle the like of which has never been offered in Germany before. A vehicle that had only one aim: highest economy and highest utility value. A vehicle that did not have its origin in the heads of engineers but rather in the potential profits the end-users will be able to make out of it. A vehicle that we don't just build to fill our capacity – that we can achieve for a long time with the Volkswagen Sedan – but in order to give the working economy a new and unique means to raise performance and profit.

The Path to Production – Nordhoff insists on the tightest of schedules

Planning for the second-generation Transporter started in 1964, three years before launch. Preparations for its successor, which debuted in the summer of 1979, were underway by 1974. By comparison, Nordhoff insisted the full process for a brand-new type of vehicle from concept to series production should take no more than a maximum of eighteen months. Approved prototypes had to be available to demonstrate to the world's press in little over a year.

Autumn 1948 – Nordhoff and Haesner met to define the essentials of a second Volkswagen model, a multi-purpose design, with an equal emphasis on the delivery of goods and the transportation of people. The outcome was Development Project – Seven (Entwicklungsauftrag, EA-7).

11 November 1948 – Haesner sent a memo to Nordhoff asking for additional staff. He wrote: 'We require the services of additional workers, as the available expertise is not adequate and effective functioning on all the projects at once is not possible.' Apart from Development Project-7, Nordhoff had demanded other tasks including a complete overhaul of the Beetle in preparation for the launch of a De Luxe or Export model in the summer of 1949.

20 November 1948 – The first two blueprints for EA-7 (Typ 29) were presented to Nordhoff. Essentially, they were the same, with the exception of the front end. Both featured a squared-off front, but one had an overhanging roof panel while the other offered a slight curve to the cab front. Nordhoff preferred the slightly curved version and, subject to satisfactory wind-tunnel tests, gave the go-ahead for a full scale prototype to be built.

7 February 1949 – Nordhoff's interest in the minutiae of the Typ 29 was becoming increasingly apparent. For example, at the February progress meeting he suggested dividing the driver's seat from that of the passengers, as it would offer the advantage of a removable bench seat. The design team later quietly rejected this idea.

9 March 1949 – The wind test report by the Institute for Flow Mechanics of the Technical College at Brunswick (Braunschweig) proved worthwhile. A model of the Transporter made of wood and to a scale of 1:10 had been fitted with three interchangeable nose shapes (bugformen). The model measured 0.383 m in length, 0.158 m in width, with the largest cross sectional area standing at 0.023 m². The wheelbase totalled 0.23 m. Neither of the two nose cones, which were best described as flat, scored well. One indicated a CW of 0.75, the other 0.77. By contrast, the rounded version, which the report referred to as being 'highly streamlined', scored a remarkable 0.43, outstanding for what was a wind resistant box on wheels.

5 April 1949 – Tests carried out under the cover of darkness on the initial prototype to assess its weight carrying abilities ended in disaster. To keep costs to a minimum, a widened Beetle chassis had been used rather than develop something specific to a vehicle that in delivery van guise was expected to carry up to 750 kg. Haesner sombrely reported: 'The results clearly

show that the task of the Typ 29, as originally conceived by Porsche amongst others, cannot be performed by the passenger car chassis, for both the load and particularly the torsion, is simply too great.' Many years later Ivan Hirst, who was still present at Wolfsburg but excluded from the Typ 29 project, told the American author Karl Ludvigsen that 'when they came back to the works in the morning the van was six inches lower. The weight of the load broke the back of the flat-section at the centre of the platform frame.'

19 May 1949 – Nordhoff announced that the Typ 29 would go into production on 1 December at the latest. He insisted that it would make its general public debut at the Geneva Motor Show to be held in March 1950. Haesner, in turn, pleaded the Typ 29 should have priority over all other projects.

Summer 1949 – A second-generation prototype had been developed with a self-supporting body, a vehicle best summarised as being of unitary construction. Essentially, the body and chassis were welded, rather than bolted, together. Two substantial longitudinal rails, supported by sturdy cross-members (or outriggers) which were welded between the front and rear axles, ensured the required structure to cope with the demands placed on this kind of vehicle. Additionally, Haesner and his team changed the ratio of total weight to un-laden weight from 1.85:1 to 1.9:1 and strengthened the front axle.

Use of the Beetle's 25PS, 1,131cc engine in the new vehicle wasn't questioned. However, as acceleration was thought to be below par, reduction gears in the rear wheel hubs were taken from the wartime cross-country vehicle, the Kübelwagen, which resulted in brisker performance and higher ground clearance. The seemingly modest top speed of 80 kph (50 mph) was perfectly acceptable by the standards of the time. Twin torsion bar spring units were used for the back axle as a cost cutting exercise.

Technical data for public release would describe the innovative forward-cab Type 29 as 'an aircraft design', by which was meant lightweight, while the summary would be of a vehicle with a 'unitized, stiff all-steel box body (with no separate chassis) with a one-piece, all-steel roof; a streamlined form with a low Cd value and the load area between the axles'.

The second prototype covered more than 12,000 km (7,460 miles) without hiccups on the factory's test track.

15 August 1949 – Nordhoff ordered four further prototypes. His deadline of 15 October was characteristically tight, but it was obvious why these later prototypes had to be on display if the concept of a multi-usage body was to be understood. His requirement was for an eight-seat minibus, a pick-up, an ambulance and a vehicle suitable for use by the German post office.

August to October 1949 – Nordhoff's persistent demands for minor improvements, both by memo and personal intervention, undoubtedly slowed progress, something he was anxious to avoid in his quest to generate substantial investment income. Changes included:

- The fuel filler was relocated from the vehicle's exterior to a more secure position within the engine compartment as petrol siphoning was rife at the time.
- Vertical cooling louvres (side panel rear) replaced with more effective horizontal ones.

- Vertical location of the spare wheel in the engine compartment was deemed to be taking too much room away from the luggage area and was replaced by a horizontal position above the engine.
- Engine bay height lowered so that an extra layer of insulation could be fitted with the aim of reducing heat from the engine.
- Stronger, redesigned and lighter weight hinges fitted to doors.
- A second wiper was added to clear the passenger screen as well as the driver's.
- Heating and ventilation were assessed and improved.

31 August – an additional prototype was added to the programme. An emphasis was placed on further road tests, the roughest of roads in Lower Saxony proving ideal for endurance trials.

9 September 1949 – Satisfactory second wind tunnel report: 1:10 scale model again (length 0.4 m, width 0.158 m, wheelbase 0.24 m, largest cross sectional area 0.252 m²). CW 0.44 (maximum wind speeds 56 m/second, previously 41.5 m/second).

26 September 1949 – Haesner was clearly under pressure as his memo to Nordhoff illustrates.

Keeping the press date for the appearance of the four models presupposes, amongst other things, that the roof panels are delivered by 10 October. We need four for the prototypes and a fifth one that we can try out first. The roof panels that have been produced so far have been made by hand, rather than being machine pressed. They can only be delivered in flat form and not curved as is required for the press models. As a result, they lack the necessary tension, with the consequence that they flutter while driving. Therefore, we must acquire curved, machine-pressed roofs for the press models.

Unfortunately for Haesner, the press works were unable to carry out the required work and there was no option but to produce the roofs by hand, a four-week undertaking.

20 October 1949 – Despite organising overtime, Haesner had to report that the roof panels still weren't ready. To Nordhoff's displeasure, the date for the press release had to be delayed to 6 November.

4 November 1949 – Haesner wrote that painting was taking longer than he had anticipated. On the same day Nordhoff despatched a handwritten note insisting that the overall weight of the vehicle must not exceed 875 kg.

The press launch was reluctantly moved to 12 November with Nordhoff making it clear that he wouldn't tolerate another postponement.

12 November 1949 – Nordhoff addressed the press. In the haste to bring the Typ 29 into production, a name for it hadn't been finalised! In addition to the prototypes on show there were handouts depicting an ambulance, a milk truck, radio and specific purpose vans. Nordhoff declared, 'This vehicle is suitable for all sectors of business, express delivery and freight transport, for example a minibus, special purpose vehicle, post van, ambulance or

mobile shop.' He emphasised the engine location and load position, using a giant diagram ready to illustrate the innovative nature of the design. 'We are not tied to the general view of technology. The famous "cab over engine" arrangement gives such terrible load distribution ratios in an empty van, that it was never an option. You can tell from the state of the roadside trees in the entire British Zone how the lorries of the English Army, which have been built according to this principle, handle when they are un-laden.'

Dr Haesner's own summary ran as follows:

> We have been assisted in the design by the requirements for a delivery van that is more or less universal: a) the vehicle has to utilise as much of the floor area as possible for cargo space; b) the Transporter has to be as versatile as possible; c) the vehicle must be available as a pick-up with a canvas top. Considering these requirements, we have developed the Typ 29 for urban and country use, for autobahns and fields, for both goods and passengers. It can be used by all small businesses and delivery firms as well as by the Bundespost and ambulance service. The Typ 29 is readily manoeuvrable and is fuel-efficient. It is robust and requires little in the way of maintenance. It is easy to load and to drive. It makes use of the latest technology and looks attractive. It is reliable in both summer and winter, and is available with a range of special equipment and features. The Typ 29 is just as much a genuine Volkswagen as the Beetle saloon, with its lively, reliable, efficient and useful features. Above all, it is a general-purpose utility vehicle.

Two press shots of the new Transporter in prototype form. Note the vertical air intake slots and the external filler cap. Neither feature made it to the production stage.

Normalausführung

To herald the Transporter's arrival, Volkswagen produced a brochure entitled 'VW Delivery Van – A series of pictures'. This prototype is less well known than some of its compatriots.

Schnell auswechselbare Sitzbänke
Personen- oder Güterbeförderung nach Wahl

The load and passenger area of the prototype VW Kombi – note the hallmark expanses of painted metal and the unusual sofa-like seating.

Above and below: The prototype Micro Bus depicts a more upmarket approach to passenger comforts than was intended for Kombi owners.

Two images despatched to the press, along with a type-written release, outlining the new production Transporter's key selling points (post-31 October 1950). The sketch is near identical to the one Nordhoff used to illustrate the revolutionary design of the vehicle at his November 1949 press conference.

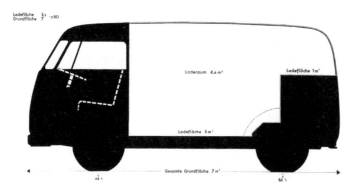

Technical Specification in 1950/1 (Simplified from One of the Earliest Micro Bus Brochures Printed)

Motor

The diminutive 25 PS air-cooled engine in its cavernous compartment. Note the petrol tank in close proximity.

Engine

Design:	4-cylinder, 4-stroke carburettor engine in the rear of the vehicle.
Cylinder arrangement:	Opposite 2-cylinder
Mass:	
Cylinder bore:	75 mm
Stroke:	64 mm
Displacement:	1,131 cm²
Compression ratio:	5.8: 1
Valves:	Overhead type
Maximum power:	25PS at 3,300 rpm
Piston speed:	6.42 m/s at 3,000 rpm
Lubrication:	Pressure circulation lubrication (gear pump) with oil cooler
Fuel Pump:	Diaphragm type
Carburettor:	Downdraught type with accelerating pump
Cooling:	Air-cooling by fan

Clutch

Type:	Single dry plate

Gears

Final Drive:	Transmission by spiral toothed bevel gearbox with bevel differential gear of swing half axles and spur reduction gears to the rear wheels. Ratio – 1:62
Gearbox:	Four forward speeds, one reverse, 3rd and 4th silent
	Gear ratios: 1st, 1:3.60 – 2nd, 1:2.07 – 3rd, 1:1.25 – 4th, 1:0.8 – Reverse, 1:6,6

Chassis

Suspension:	Front: Two solid square leaf spring bars.
	Rear: One round pivot rod on each side.
Shock absorber:	Front and rear hydraulic, double acting.
Smallest turning circle diameter:	Approximately 11 m.
Foot brake:	Hydraulic brake (Ate), acting on four wheels.
Hand brake:	Mechanical acting on the rear wheels.
Wheels:	16-inch
Tyres:	5.50–16
Wheelbase:	2,400 mm
Track width:	Front 1,356 mm, rear 1,360 mm
Mass:	
Length:	4,100 mm
Width:	1,660 mm
Height:	1,900 mm
Ground clearance:	285 mm
Passenger Compartment:	
Length:	2.00 m

Width:	1.50 m
Height:	1.35 m
Number of seats:	Eight
'Luggage Room':	
Length:	0.70 m
Width:	1.50 m
Height:	0.55 m

Weights

Net Weight, including tank filled up:	1,045 kg
Weight (filled) with spare wheel and accessories:	1,070 kg
Permitted load:	715 kg
Gross vehicle weight:	1,750 kg

Fuel

Fuel tank:	40 litres, including a 5-litre reserve
Fuel consumption:	Approximately 9½ litres / 100 km (road usage)

Performance

Continuous top speed:	75 km/h at 3,100 RPM
Hill Climbing Ability:	First speed: 23%, Second speed: 13%, Third speed: 7%, Fourth speed: 3.5%

PS - a word or two please

While PS might suggest an additional note or afterthought to avid letter or memo writers, in automotive parlance the initials represent metric horsepower, as they stand for the word *Pferdestärken*. Usage of PS avoids the confusion that arises when referring to brake horsepower, as there is a variance in measured value between American bhp SAE and British bhp DIN, the former suggesting greater power than the latter. From 1972 onwards, SAE calculations, as used by the US motor manufacturing industry, changed once more. To reassure British readers, the variance between bhp DIN and PS is minimal: simply multiply the PS value by 0.986.

Developing a Range of Micro-Buses and Commercial Transporters

Setting the Scene

In the first-generation Transporter's near seventeen-year production run, first at Wolfsburg and later at its own purpose-built factory in Hanover, sales totalled 1,833,000 before a new model took over the reins in August of 1967. However, satellite factory production in Brazil, which continued until 1975, added another 400,000 distinctive examples (see epilogue), while South African- and Australian-built vehicles, the latter known as Kombis whatever the model, accounted for a further 35,000 RHD vehicles. Although compared to the phenomenon that was the VW Beetle, where sales exceeded more than half of the Transporter's total production run for the first time in 1965, the box-on-wheels's production figures might appear sedate, in reality its success was unprecedented for a vehicle of its type. Apart from the Transporter's ground-breaking characteristics when it was launched, the diversity of models planned from the start and that rapidly developed ensured its appeal to the widest possible spectrum of the motoring population.

Mass production of the Transporter, if such it can be called, started on 8 March 1950 at a less than shattering rate of ten Delivery Vans per day. Previously, during February, one or two vehicles had been produced which were bequeathed to good customers. The Delivery Van might have been first out of the pod, helping to establish its significance, but on 16 May the revolutionary dual-purpose and aptly named Kombi joined it, while just a few days later, on 22 May, production of the more up-market Micro Bus began. The potential to offer model diversity was plain for all to see, a principle demonstrated in the progression from practical goods-carrying metal shell and little else, to a vehicle with side windows and basic, easily removable seating for all the family, and then to a fully trimmed and upholstered precursor to today's people carriers.

The Delivery Van

Taking even a short journey in an early Delivery Van is an ear-shattering experience, even shouted conversation between driver and passenger proving virtually impossible. The almost complete lack of any form of insulation or trim and the clatter of the always noisy air-cooled engine provide the key ingredients for the antithesis of peace and quiet. Spartan cab accoutrements in the form of a plain, un-adjustable bench seat; provision of a single binnacle and no dashboard to provide all the information a driver may need during a journey; a smattering of basic fibreboard panels; a distinct lack of ventilation and ineffective and potentially fume enhanced heating taken direct off the engine, all serve to suggest sales might well be repressed due to the specification. The load area offered no niceties; bare metal and metal which lacked a gloss finish and any form of protective cladding were abundant. The floor of the load area followed the same minimalistic specification.

However, it should be remembered that rival manufactures offered nothing better in terms of luxury, their offerings, at least initially, suffering from the defects any car-turned-into-a-van might have, particularly the age-old problem of weight distribution and consequent poor handling. The carefully balanced layout of the Delivery Van, with weight almost equally

Above and opposite: Dating from 1954, the Delivery Van shown here is a very early example of a RHD vehicle. Painted in ubiquitous Dove Blue externally and the equivalent of grey primer inside, a lack of sound deadening insulation is apparent. Note the size of the engine lid particularly, which led to pre-March 1955 Transporters being nicknamed 'barn-door' models by later enthusiasts; the lack of a dashboard – its place being taken by a single binnacle; and a revised location (from 31 October 1950) for the spare wheel on a platform (compare picture on p. 18). The twin side loading doors (two to the left, two to the right), were an extra cost option available from 27 June 1951.

As you look towards the rear of the Delivery Van's load area it is obvious how obtrusive the large engine bay was.

distributed between driver and passengers at the front and the engine and gearbox at the rear, ensured much better handling than average and safer motoring.

However, the engine's location, and more significantly the cavernous compartment in which it was housed, precluded loading from the rear of the vehicle. The lack of any form of hatch was deemed more-or-less irrelevant even by the fastidious Nordhoff. Volkswagen's infant marketing department wrote at length about the advantages of generous double side-loading doors and the convenience of being able to pile goods into the vehicle direct from the safety of the pavement. They also pointed out that less space was required when parking on a busy high street between the rear of the VW and the next vehicle, which had no doubt already tried to squeeze into a small space as the only one available.

Nevertheless, the inconvenience of a lack of rear doors, or a loading hatch, was neatly illustrated when the coachbuilders Miesen created an ambulance version of the Kombi in the latter months of 1950. Loading a patient on a stretcher through the side doors was clearly far from easy and involved shuffling the patient to-and-fro before a dash to the hospital could be made. A partial solution to the problem was obvious, necessitating a reduction in the size of the engine compartment, a feat achieved with Volkswagen's own version of the Ambulance launched in December 1951.

The Kombi

Without doubt the Kombi was a clever introduction, a genuine first and a concept that would soon be annexed by many other manufacturers. Although it might be hard to imagine in these bountiful days of multi-car ownership and 'works' vehicles, many a small business in 1950s Germany and elsewhere, fledgling or otherwise, could not afford the essential Delivery Van for usage during the week and the luxury of a car for leisure-time activities on Sundays. The Kombi offered a solution to this dilemma. Essentially a Delivery

Van with windows and 'load compartment' seating, the ingenuity of the concept ensured its place as the second most popular model in the range after its blank-sided sibling.

All Volkswagen's designers had to do was take a tin-opener to both side-loading doors and the corresponding panel to the rear of this and match what had been done with three further openings on the long plain side of the Delivery Van. Incidentally, the Delivery Van, Kombi and Micro Bus lacked any form of rear window until April 1951.

In terms of fixtures and fittings, those allocated to the Kombi were few and far between. Like the Delivery Van, it had a plain hardboard headlining in the cab, fibreboard door panels and a simple rubber floor mat. Differing from the Delivery Van, this matting extended to the load-come-passenger area, but in all other respects the two types were identical. To confirm, the Kombi had no headlining in the seating-come-load area, nor was there anything other than bare metal surrounding the windows or below the waistline – austerity-driven bare painted metal was the order of the day. The load area seating was similar in nature to that in the cab, albeit more generously padded. The frame was of a simple metal nature, whilst removing the seats couldn't have been easier as wing nuts secured them to the floor.

The marketing men added one further somewhat contrived dimension to the Kombi's assets. The ploy was to proclaim the side windows as ideal advertising vessels when the vehicle was in use as a workhorse. Perhaps some people, sceptical concerning many an advertising person's wilder schemes, might have wondered how many owners of Kombis opted to place adverts against the glass during the week and remove them at a weekend.

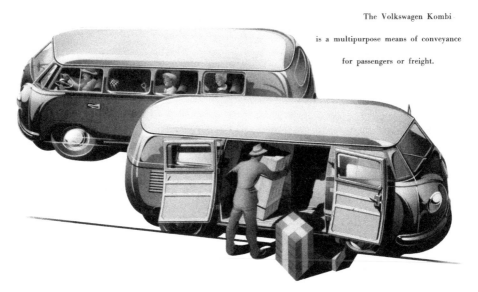

The artist Bernd Reuters illustrated the dual role of the Kombi in a manner guaranteed to catch the eye.

The seats can be removed in no time to transform the Volkswagen Kombi into a handsome and practical delivery truck.

The very basic nature of the Kombi for passengers is apparent in this early brochure image which reveals large expanses of painted metal and little else.

The Micro Bus

Hot on the heels of the Kombi came the Micro Bus or *Kleinbus*, later to be known as the Station Wagon in the USA and in Germany, for a time at least, as the *Sieben* or *Achtsitzer*. In comparison to the Delivery Van and the Kombi, the Micro Bus oozed both comfort and quality, even if in keeping with a modern jaundiced view of the era, the Bus still appears remarkably primitive. Indicative of the specification, the Micro Bus sported a full-length cloth headlining, which extended to the areas around the side windows, while acres of bare metal were banned and replaced by elegantly trimmed panels complete with anodised alloy mouldings. Banished were the plain vinyl bench-seats in favour of upholstery that was both fluted and piped, whilst being fixed in the passenger area in a way that made it more permanent in nature. Seeming trivialities, such as the equivalent of modesty boards shrouding the nether regions of the middle row of seats, and an abundance of ashtrays, were significant at the time, as was the elegant (but rigid) division between the lesser ranks occupying the cab seat and those conveyed in luxury behind. In similar vein the rear side windows could be opened, while the hubcaps were favoured with a chrome finish. Finally, without delving towards obscurity, for the first time at launch a Transporter was

A pre-March 1955 Micro Bus finished in Brown Beige and Light Beige.

In an age when promoting any VW was normally placed in the hands of an artist, this photograph of a Micro Bus is one of a series of carefully composed shots contained in the brochure *Volkswagenwerk presents its products,* which was published in 1952.

offered with two-tone paintwork, namely Brown Beige over Light Beige, although a single colour option, not a shade available for either the Kombi or the Delivery Van, provided a second choice.

From a marketing point of view and taking the lead set by Nordhoff back in 1949, the aim was to portray the Micro Bus as a car with a larger carrying capacity, as the following short extract from a US market brochure serves to illustrate:

> The Volkswagen Micro Bus is in reality not a bus but an oversize car accommodating eight persons. Every passenger has more head, leg and elbow room than he needs...

The Micro Bus De Luxe

Just over a year after the launch of Micro Bus, when, first, Volkswagen had started to amass more in the way of reserves and, second, the post-war economy was undoubtedly showing much more definite signs of bursting into sturdy growth, Nordhoff added a further core model to the Transporter range, a significantly more upmarket people carrier, appropriately given the title of De Luxe as well as Micro Bus. Amongst modern-day enthusiasts this version of the Transporter, endearingly nicknamed the Samba, is by far the most popular model from the split-window era. Original and fully restored examples command significant sums of money. By way of contrast, in its day the Samba was far less popular than its cheaper sibling, annual sales never approaching even 50 per cent of those of the Micro Bus. Although the De Luxe proved popular with airlines and hotels, for example, who wished to ferry passengers between destinations in a modicum of comfort, for many an individual the premium price asked was one step too far, or for others the Micro Bus was sufficient. A pricelist dating from 1954 indicates a cost of DM 6,600 for

This glorious picture of the Micro Bus De Luxe, which cleverly infers the pleasure of luxury and leisure combined with the vehicle's ability to carry an extended family, was probably taken in 1951 as the roof panel painted white was theoretically restricted to pre-production vehicles. The image takes centre stage in the 1952 publication, *Volkswagenwerk presents its products.*

a fully fledged Kombi (by then it could be purchased with or without seats in the 'load' area), DM 6,975 for the Micro Bus and a hefty DM 8,475 for the De Luxe offering. Even the hand-crafted luxury Beetle Cabriolet cost nearly DM 2,000 less than the Samba.

At least two features of the new De Luxe model's specification help to illustrate that, increasingly, every opportunity was taken to offer as many options as possible. The Micro Bus De Luxe came as standard with a full-length, fold-back canvas sunroof, manufactured by the German firm Golde. One of Volkswagen's most inspirational sales brochures of the time depicted the De Luxe with its sunroof open and its passengers delighting in the open-air motoring this afforded. The artist Bernd Reuters, renowned for his flattering, stylised interpretations of Volkswagens and previously many other brands, streamlined the appearance of the stolid De Luxe, giving it believable curves which didn't exist, adding air lines that implied speeds which the vehicle was incapable of, making it appear particularly spacious by reducing the proportions of its occupants against the length, width and height of the body, while giving a gloss to the paintwork even modern-day techniques often fail to deliver. Without doubt though, the Micro Bus De Luxe's sunroof was the focal point of his work, a luxury that set the lifestyle tone for the vehicle.

Above and overleaf pages: This early Micro Bus De Luxe is particularly rare in that it lacks both the canvas sunroof and the roof skylights, something very few potential owners opted for. Finished externally in iconic Chestnut Brown over Sealing Wax Red, the interior is largely original. The early speedometer appears to run backwards, while both it and the clock are features of the Samba only dashboard. The curved rear corner window is 'glazed' with Plexiglas, a cheaper option at the time than normal glass. Note the much larger rear window allocated to the De Luxe and the half-hearted attempt to protect the bodywork with the makings of a rear bumper.

The sales ploy was to offer the sunroof as a factory-fitted extra cost option to would-be purchasers of the Micro Bus who either couldn't afford the fully-fledged luxury of the De Luxe, or who simply wanted semi open-air motoring. To complete the circle, if the would-be buyer of a De Luxe didn't wish to benefit from fresh air or sunshine, an admittedly rare decision, the De Luxe could be specified without the sunroof and the accompanying roof lights so far not mentioned.

A second feature unique to the Samba as a standard item was a full-length dashboard. All other models, as has been mentioned, came with a single binnacle housing the rudimentary instrumentation of the day. Although spartan by today's standards, the De Luxe dashboard was of an elegant, symmetrical design and accommodated a large clock, chromed ashtray and a blanking panel for the insertion of a radio. Like the Golde sunroof, the dashboard too could be specified as an extra cost option for the Micro Bus (as an aside while discussing dashboards, when the entire Transporter range was granted a facelift in March 1955, all models benefited from a full-length dashboard. Sadly for Samba owners, their dash was of the same design as that fitted to the 'also-rans'!)

The list of features that distinguish the De Luxe from its lesser sibling is near endless and ranges from the significant to the trivial. Upholstery was refined and fittings finished in an ivory colour, rather than ubiquitous black. This extended to the steering wheel, which also carried a Wolfsburg crest design on the horn push-button. At the back of the vehicle the luggage area was carpeted, and bars or rails were fitted against the windows to avoid the risk of damage to the glass, a subject to be discussed further shortly.

Externally, the Micro Bus De Luxe featured bright trim strips which ran along the belt line and down the V swage line of the front panel. The bumpers were similarly adorned

Above and below: This classic twenty-three-window Samba, complete with a rear bumper, dates to a point after 10 March 1953 when such an item was fitted to the De Luxe model only.

with additional trim, although originally the Samba was the only model to have any form of protection, never mind sturdy bumpers, at the rear, while both the hubcaps and the large VW roundel at the front were chromed. Although the De Luxe (in the early years) was available in a single-colour finish, the exclusive and very attractive combination of Sealing Wax Red paint under Chestnut Brown upper panels was synonymous with the model.

One further significant feature distinguishes the Micro Bus De Luxe from its lowlier brethren. A modern-day Samba owner is likely to slip into enthusiast speak and say he, or she, owns a twenty-three or twenty-one window Bus dependent on the year it was built. Owners of other passenger carrying models are less likely to refer to their vehicle's eleven windows (three down each side, one at the rear, two cab door windows and the split windscreen – total eleven). The De Luxe sported an extra window towards the rear of the vehicle on either side, two wrap-round windows, one at each rear corner, and four skylights on either side of the roof. These last-mentioned items and the corner windows were made from Plexiglas, at the time a cheaper option than curved glass. Plexiglas was a Perspex-type material often used in the manufacture of canopies for aeroplane cockpits (in February 1955, tempered safety glass, by then less expensive to consider and less prone to becoming scratched or prematurely aged if exposed to the elements, became a part of the standard specification). Finally, the rear window was much larger than that allocated to other models at the time. The result was the lightest and airiest of interiors and particularly so when the sunroof was open too. (Glass or Plexiglas towards the rear of the vehicle and abutting the luggage area situated above the intrusively large engine bay demanded those rails or bars previously referenced.)

A pre-production lifestyle image of the Micro Bus De Luxe attempting to justify the cost of luxury appointments and sunroof motoring.

The Ambulance

Six months hence, yet another model made its debut; a seemingly niche market option that nevertheless would be included in literature covering all the key versions of the Transporter for a good number of years to come. Perhaps Director General Nordhoff was insistent; after all he had spoken about vehicles of the same ilk, such as a Bus devoted to Post Office usage. He possibly saw this low overall potential for rivalling any other model in the core range (in sales) as more of a demonstrator for what was possible.

Passing reference has already been made to the coachbuilders Miesen and their Transporter-based ambulance and the difficulties of 'loading' patients through the double side-doors, due to that lack of an opening at the rear of the vehicle. Volkswagen's in-house solution to this failing was to create an ambulance with rear loading facilities. The design and tooling expenditure would not have been trivial, yet, curiously, having achieved what was required, the improvement was not rolled out to the rest of the range for a further three-plus years, and only then as part of a more general facelift for the six-year-old design.

To make room for a rear door, initially hinged at the top but not many months later redesigned to open downwards, thus providing an extra surface on which to ease a patient into the vehicle, the size of the engine compartment had to be reduced. As there was copious space surrounding the diminutive air-cooled power plant, lowering the compartment's 'ceiling' shouldn't have presented a problem. However, as the spare wheel was sited on a tray above the engine and the fuel tank apparently precariously to its left side, the task was more complicated. The former found a home behind the cab bench-seat, while the latter was relocated out of sight and under the fabric of the vehicle – above and to the right of the gearbox. The fuel filler pipe and cap, hidden away within the engine compartment on other models, was now located behind a little trap door to the rear of the short side panel (itself behind the two side-loading doors) – a far more sensible option.

One of a series of three late model press images of the Ambulance designed for the British market to savour. There is no evidence to suggest the NHS succumbed and bought in bulk!

The paraphernalia associated with the transportation of patients, both seated and prone, and the storage of medical equipment and supplies were outlined in Volkswagen's Transporter range brochures and model specific material.

During the production run of the first-generation Transporter, annual sales of the Ambulance generally hovered around the 650 mark per annum, peaking at 883 in 1961. In the same year over 45,000 Delivery Vans were produced, the Pick-up took the second prize, accounting for nearly 37,000 units.

Above and right: Note both the frosted glass to maintain a patient's privacy and how the rear hatch is hinged at its base to facilitate loading a stretcher.

The Pick-up

Well justified expenditure to create the Pick-up led to the model's debut as part of the Transporter range in August 1952, just eight months after the Ambulance. The cavernous engine bay, bequeathed to the Delivery Van et al., was clearly inappropriate for a vehicle specifically created to have a readily accessible loading platform. However, the money spent on creating a suitably compacted home for the engine in the Ambulance now made much more sense, as did the 'new' position for the fuel tank.

Nevertheless, there was work to be done to create a versatile Pick-up, whether it was in the development of an appropriate drop-down tail and side gates, or in the highly valuable 1.9 m² lockable, and therefore secure, area for storage of items vulnerable to light fingers.

Launched on 25 August 1952, early Pick-ups (models produced before 11 November 1953) lacked reinforcing mouldings in the side and tail gates.

Unintentionally, this battered but largely rust-free barn door era Pick-up highlights the secure storage area below the main loading platform.

This carefully posed press image was designed to illustrate the load platform's convenient height and, no doubt, to note how the Pick-up lends itself to conveying items unsuited to the Delivery Van.

Ambulance technology played its part again when it came to allocating a place for the spare wheel, although the cost of tooling for a truncated roof panel covering the cab had to be met.

The Double Cab Pick-up

When no further major introductions emerged from Wolfsburg's inner portals in not just 1953 but the next few years too, some commentators assumed that Volkswagen's ability to diversify in relation to the Transporter had all but dried up. They were wrong on two counts. Beneath the headline models a myriad of niche market, specific trade-related variations on the core models were emerging, the early days Ambulance by coachbuilders Miesen being an obvious example. Previous references to the versatility of the Kombi and the ideas it provoked in, for instance, the coachbuilder Westfalia's boardroom hint at further offerings. The second count, however, was conclusive. The arrival of a further major model on 3 November 1958, a Transporter variant destined to sell well and particularly so in the United States, settled the matter.

The new model from the Hanover stable was the Double Cab Pick-up, a versatile combination of a Transporter with the ability to seat up to six people in reasonable comfort,

Above and below: Two pictures of beautifully restored versatile Double Cab Pick-ups, noble precursors to the VW Amarok, caught on camera at a vintage VW gathering in Germany. Both suggest room for five passengers and the driver, secure storage under the passenger area bench seat, and ample space for loading goods unsuited to other vehicles in the range.

but also carry the kind of materials and goods on its flatbed that were considered unsuited to the Delivery Van.

The Lorch Württemberg-based coachbuilders Binz & Co. had successfully created their version of a Double Cab in October 1953. They purchased Pick-ups direct from Wolfsburg (and later Hanover), cut off the rear of the cab, relocating it 85 cm further back, fitted a new extended roof panel and added both a bulkhead panel and a rear side door. The standard of work was generally rather crude, but the concept worked sufficiently well to entice would-be owners both in Germany and, more significantly for Volkswagen, in the United States to part with the additional DM 895 the conversion cost.

Volkswagen's annexation of the Double Cab was a logical development. The factory-produced version, as might be expected, was finished to a much higher standard. Obvious signs of welding were no longer the case, while the access door to the rear bench seat opened conventionally (as opposed to Binz's suicide style) and included Volkswagen's normal means of opening its window. Ingeniously, even though the single cab Pick-up's secure storage area under the loading platform was lost through the inclusion of a double cab, an enclosed space was created under the rear bench seat to compensate.

Being a favourite of the construction trade might explain a relatively low survival rate.

The High Roof Delivery Van

September 1961 saw the arrival of what is generally regarded as the last core range model, a high-roof version of the Delivery Van. This was still largely a time when materials other than metal were deemed inferior, so, quite simply, the new model's panels above the swage line were extended until trades such as the garment industry knew that they could hang full length dresses without fear of them crumpling or creasing as they swept the floor. The most complex panel was the curved one which sat above the split windowpanes at the front of the vehicle, but even this would hardly have tested the design department's ingenuity. At the rear, a simple blanking panel sat above what was the standard arrangement of hatch and engine compartment lid. Taller side loading doors completed the picture. Nevertheless, for the privilege of all but the tallest of people being able to stand up in the high-roof version of the Delivery Van, a premium price which added some 24 per cent to the cost of a standard model was demanded (GB, 1967 – Delivery Van £680, High Roof £910).

Above and opposite: The slightly ungainly High Roof Delivery Van was made entirely out of steel, unlike later models with fibreglass panels. Note that at its rear the standard hatch prevails, with extra tin-ware above in a form equivalent to a blanking panel, thus avoiding the need to create more special panels. This example is something of a rarity, as it features extra-cost sliding doors.

More Transporters

Sales brochures dating from the mid-1960s frequently include an equal allocation of space to Transporters that are not included in the definition of the core range. For example, the Delivery Van was available with both left and right side-loading doors from the end of June 1951, while the option of a sliding door (as per standard on the second-generation Transporter) was offered from mid-April 1963. A 1964 US market brochure devotes a double page spread to the 'VW Delivery Van with sliding doors'. In the same manner, while an equal amount of space is allocated to both the Pick-up and the Double Cab Pick-up as might be expected, it is also given to the self-explanatory 'VW Pick-up with enlarged platform'.

As Nordhoff had realised from the start, the key to the Transporter's success was in its diversity of models. Producing a Delivery Van and nothing else, however revolutionary, would have been futile. With the possible exception of the Ambulance, every variant manufactured in the VW factory, first at Wolfsburg and later at Hanover, could be regarded as equally significant as the other: each a mass production, profit-earning model. Providing coachbuilders didn't do anything to dent Volkswagen's reputation it was logical to develop a list of approved or licensed firms, each of which would provide models that were sufficiently specialist in nature for them not to be economic for the VW factory to produce itself. And on that basis, what did it matter if space in brochures was allocated to vehicles that were neither specialist, nor simply basic standard spec?

Highlights of a Seventeen-Year History

In the first-generation Transporter's lengthy seventeen-year production span there were three occasions that stand above all others. The first, which occurred in March 1955, saw the Transporter given more than a makeover. Indeed, Nordhoff would never have sanctioned changes of a purely cosmetic nature. The second, the opening of a new factory dedicated to Transporter production and engine assembly, took place on 8 March 1956, with full production following on 20 April. The third, the arrival of the millionth Transporter, was marked on 20 September 1962.

An Era of Continual Improvement

As Nordhoff reached and then passed the customary age for retirement, a growing number of journalists and politicians started to question his model policy and particularly so with regard to the Beetle, which in 1965 could be declared a thirty-year-old design. Nordhoff's answer had been composed as long ago as 1958. He was in America to collect the Elmer A. Sperry award, presented to Volkswagen for their significant contribution to transportation. In the course of his lengthy address, Nordhoff outlined why he had acted as he had done in the context of the Beetle. However, his words remain just as relevant to the first-generation Transporter and explain why its production run extended to a period of over seventeen years.

> I brushed away all the temptations to change model and design. In any sound design there are almost unlimited possibilities – and this was certainly a sound one. I see no sense in starting anew every few years with the same teething troubles, making obsolete all the past. I went out on a limb. I took the chance of breaking away from the beaten path ...
>
> Offering people an honest value, a product of highest quality, with low original cost and incomparable re-sale value, appealed more to me than being driven around by a batch of hysterical stylists trying to sell something they really do not want to have.
>
> I am firmly convinced that there will always be a market in this world, which we are far from covering now, for simple, economical and dependable transportation and for an honest value in performance and quality ... There are millions of people

who will gladly exchange chromium plated gadgets and excessive power for economy, long life and inexpensive maintenance.

So I have decided to stick to the policy that has served us so well ... The Volkswagen of today looks almost exactly like the prototype model ... but every single part of this [vehicle] has been refined and improved over the years - these will continue to be our "model changes".

The Transporter Year-by-Year Without a Single Reference to a Widget

9 October 1950 – Micro Bus – heating available for passenger area.
11 November 1950 – Large VW badge on rear of vehicle deleted (at this stage no models had a rear window, a characteristic of many a white van nowadays. However, in early Transporter thinking, a rear window was simply deemed un-necessary, while today the main purpose might be considered a theft deterrent).
20 April 1951 – Rear window fitted.

The earliest of Transporters – pre-11 November 1950 – featured a prominent VW symbol on the windowless rear panel.

The rear window made its debut in April 1951 (note, the bumper trim is an addition to the standard specification).

43

Painting the Transporter's Portrait

During 1951, the already well-known and respected commercial artist Bernd Reuters produced a series of spectacular images of the various models of Transporter then available. Most were designed to adorn the front cover of sales brochures, whether slender four-page affairs devoted to a single type, or more extravagant multi-page presentations where the artwork was similarly more evocative. Reuters offered an atmospheric scene with the Transporter as a focal point, rather than a study of the vehicle with little in the way of background. For the next few years Reuters added to his work, be it in the shape of a study of an additional model, or with a further inspirationally glossy scene. Similarly, as improvements were made by Volkswagen to the standard specification, Reuters modified his work.

In the spirit of the time, Reuters was particularly adept at exaggerating the size and streamlining the lines of the Transporter. Driver and passenger would invariably be smaller in proportion to the scale of the vehicle than reality, making both the passenger seating areas and cab appear more spacious. Equally, the appeal of fresh air motoring would be stressed with a Micro Bus De Luxe sunroof that left very little of the vehicle's roof panel to glossy metal, while a fantasy feeling of speed was created by 'air lines' which rushed their way across the Transporter's wheels and, on occasion, its lower body.

Bernd Reuters created a series of magnificent portraits of the Transporter in its various guises in the early 1950s, modifying some as changes in specification occurred. Here is the Micro Bus. Note the spacious cab (achieved by altering the scale of the occupants), the subtly elongated body, the enhanced, curvaceous front panel, the depth of shine in the paintwork and, of course, the air lines implying a speed rarely, if ever, attained.

Right: Victor Mundorff, another artist like Reuters, well known in the motoring world at the time, contributed a series of paintings which set a given model of Transporter against its ideal environment. Mundorff's images were not intended to offer an accurate representation, or any great detail, of the vehicle painted.

Below: Robert Preis started to illustrate the Transporter for publicity purposes shortly after the face-lift of March 1955. Some of his images replicated the positions of vehicles adopted by Reuters, but few would suggest they are simply copies.

VW-Sieben- oder Achtsitzer „Sonder-Modell"

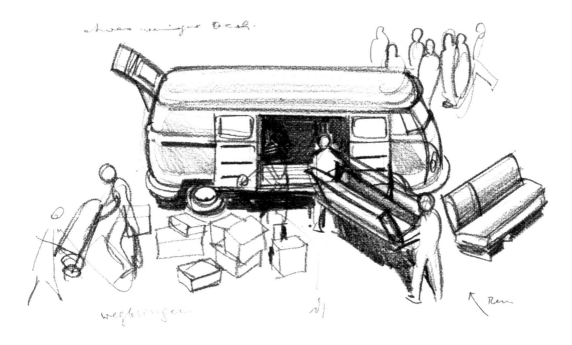

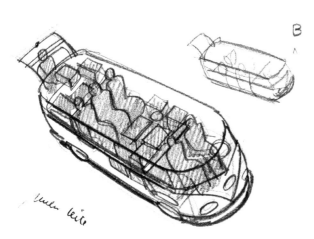

Above and left: A rare glimpse of Preis's original pencil sketches, which convey how he drafted what he perceived the best image of a Transporter for approval, before progressing to both detail and colour. The versatility of the Kombi and carrying capabilities of the Micro Bus are the assumed themes here.

Shortly after the Transporter revamp of March 1955, Reuters handed his Transporter mantle over to his fellow artist Robert Preis. His style was more conservative, his vehicles showing fewer signs of deviation from reality; nevertheless it was intended to convey an image of the Transporter that a photograph could not provide.

Whether sales brochures of the era and the work of Reuters, particularly, generated additional sales can neither be proved nor disproved, but no history of the first-generation Transporter would be complete without reference to two of the most talented artists of the era.

2 January 1953 – Re-design of cab quarter lights allowing more air to circulate in the vehicle. Today blowers, fans and air-conditioning cocoon us, but for many years, the quarter light was an integral part of a vehicle's make up. With the quarter light open and angled to direct air into the cab as the vehicle was moving, it proved an effective way of cooling a vehicle in summer. Opening quarter lights also helped with the early Transporter's perennial problem of steaming-up on wet or cold winter days. The redesign might suggest that this was a major issue which, as can be seen by the changes made to the Transporter in March 1955, it was!

10 March 1953 – Rear bumper fitted to the Micro Bus De Luxe (until this point no Transporter had a rear bumper).

10 March 1953 – Synchromesh for second, third and fourth gear. During the 1950s and earlier, it was not uncommon for a driver to have to double-declutch to change gear, a skill which, when mastered, became second nature.

10 March 1953 – Behr air scoop available as a service part (this device relieved the constant battle of steamed up cab windows – see March 1955).

21 Dec 1953 – Engine upgraded from 25 PS (1,131cc) to 30 PS (1,192cc). Today, when we would anticipate a Transporter to sport over 100 PS, we might think Volkswagen totally unrealistic to have installed such a small engine in the vehicle. Yes, performance was pedestrian, and throughout its production run, nought to 60 kph figures were rarely quoted (the 25 PS engine had a top speed of 80 km/h (50 mph) and it took 22.7 seconds to achieve 0–65 km/h (0–40 mph). However, values have changed and at the time VW proved perfectly competitive with the engines they offered.

A partial solution to the problem of ventilation – the officially recognised Behr air-scoop can be seen attached to the roof above the windscreen.

9 October 1954 and the occasion of the production of the 100,000th Transporter – Nordhoff was on hand to say more than a few words.

21 Dec 1953 – All models except the Pick-up now fitted with a rear bumper.

1 April 1954 – The Pick-up joins the other models, as it now has a rear bumper.

1 April 1954 – The Ambulance is fitted with a fuel gauge. The rest of the range continue to rely on a reserve tank operated by a flip switch when the gauge-less vehicle started to cough, spit and splutter. Although Volkswagen was somewhat tardy in specifying a fuel gauge as standard (see July 1961), it was not an uncommon feature of 1950s and earlier motoring.

9 Oct 1954 – Less than five years after Transporter production started, Wolfsburg celebrated as the 100,000th vehicle left the Wolfsburg assembly line. A sign of escalating sales was that 40,119 of the 100,000 were produced in 1954.

18 Feb 1955 – Micro Bus De Luxe curved rear corner windows now made out of glass, previously Plexiglas (similar to Perspex). Curved glass was prohibitively expensive to produce in earlier years, hence the use of 'plastic'. This also helps to explain why the first-generation Transporter featured a split-screen windscreen (one of its most endearing features nowadays).

4 March 1955 – The last of the so-called barn-door Transporters, the pre revamp vehicles, left the Wolfsburg assembly line.

The Revamped Transporter of March 1955

Without doubt, Nordhoff was in a hurry to see the Transporter make its debut once he had taken the decision to go ahead with a second model and Alfred Haesner had been appointed development manager. Despite Nordhoff's frequent interventions, invariably with sound suggestions for improvements that could be made to the specification, once the first production models left the assembly line it was realised that a series of design defects had escaped the net.

Despite a concerted campaign by the marketing department to convince would-be buyers that with side-loading doors providing easy access to the pavement, the lack of rearward access was unimportant, Volkswagen's hierarchy came to realise otherwise. Similarly, the facility to circulate fresh air to the cab and beyond, preventing condensation particularly on cold, wet days, was virtually non-existent. As a consequence, a torrent of complaints hit dealers and Wolfsburg alike, something that had to be rectified. Behind the scenes there could well have been concern regarding the wastefully large engine compartment, which also contained the spare wheel and the fuel tank. The former might not have been an issue; the latter and its proximity to heat certainly was.

It is possible, at least initially, that insufficient cash reserves prevented a revamp. With regard to ventilation, a low-cost improvement was tried first. From 2 January 1953, the old-style piano-hinged quarter lights were replaced by more effective pivoting units. In at least partial admission of defeat, from 10 March of the same year the Behr air scoop became available as a service part. The following January the same scoop became a standard fitment on all Ambulances.

Of the ailments suffered by the original version of the Transporter, often known as the barn-door bus thanks to the enormous size of its engine lid, all but the ventilation issues were cured with the creation of the Ambulance, which launched less than two years after the original Delivery Van. Similarly, when the Pick-up was added to the list of core models, in terms of concept alone, the flatbed precluded any notion of a cavernous engine bay, or any location for the fuel tank other than one tucked away under the body. Why such a perfectionist as Nordhoff opted to leave the other models more or less untouched until 3 March 1955, more than three full years after the Ambulance, remains something of a mystery.

Visually, the revised specification Transporter had a new look at both the front and rear. Dealing with the latter first, all models benefitted from the Ambulance/Pick-up design changes regarding the size of the engine compartment and the location of the fuel tank and spare wheel.

To confirm, the fuel tank was reshaped so that it was flatter in profile. Its new location was above and to the right of the gearbox. It was obviously no longer possible to lift the engine lid and see the fuel filler cap and neck. The latter was re-routed through to the right-hand side of the Transporter's body. Rather than make the cap temptingly visible, it was concealed by a hinged flap. The fuel cap had a diameter of 60 mm, compared to the overly wide 80 mm of the previous incarnation. The spare wheel was relocated to the cab and housed in a purpose-constructed well, positioned behind the bench seat's backrest.

Although the most obvious advantage of reducing the size of the engine compartment was to allow rearward access in the form of a hatch, those eager to cram their Delivery Van with goods now had 4.8 cubic metres to play with (as opposed to 4.6 cubic metres). To the rear of the load area, what had once been a glorified shelf was now fully usable, even where bigger parcels, boxes and crates were involved. Those purchasing a people carrier version of the Transporter were likewise blessed with more luggage space. This proved particularly beneficial when seating up to eight individuals and above, as it was no longer necessary to manoeuvre bags and cases over the back seat – luggage could be easily loaded through the rear hatch.

Above, below and opposite: Although this Kombi (converted to a Moortown Campahome) dates from the early months of 1963, and there are differences to the specification compared with that of an immediate post-March 1955 model, it nevertheless epitomises the improvements made to the barn-door model, which transformed the overall appearance of all Transporters. Note, particularly, the peaked roof panel, designed to disguise the external elements of the new ventilation system, the much smaller engine compartment lid and the attendant and very useful hatch to access goods and chattels from the rear of the vehicle.

The new, smaller engine lid featured two hinges, while the hatch had a continuous piano style hinge. Both lid and hatch were supported by a stay.

Transferring to the front of the vehicle and the cab, the privilege of a full-length dashboard, previously exclusive in standard form to the Micro Bus De Luxe, was extended to all ranks. As previously, the dashboard was made entirely of metal, although the design was noticeably different to what had gone before, being more utilitarian in appearance, yet more practical in application. Sadly, although there were improvements such as a binnacle-mounted ignition switch and column-positioned indicator stalk, other aspects, such as a less elegant two-spoke steering wheel and the loss of the passenger grab handle, detracted slightly from the overall effect.

Fortunately, such minor niggles merged into the background for at long last there was far greater a chance that both the driver and passengers could actually see through the screen and cab side windows on a damp, humid day as Volkswagen had finally addressed the issue of adequate ventilation. To engineer what was required, the front of the Transporter had a different profile, the forward edge of the roof losing its elegant but small swage line in favour of a not unattractive peak, reminiscent of the proverbial flat cap. This protrusion above the windscreen was really an air scoop, which pushed air through a mesh gauze into a steel box fixed to the underside of the cab roof. The driver, or front seat passenger, could regulate how much air was released into the vehicle. With immediate effect promotional material included graphic explanatory drawings splattered with arrows indicating movement of air, while the accompanying text claimed that, providing the Transporter was in motion, the ventilation system was 'capable of renewing the total volume of air once every minute.'

Compliant with Volkswagen's policy of continual improvement, applicable to both the Beetle and the Transporter, a series of more minor practical improvements, none of them simply styling gimmicks preferred by most other manufacturers, completed the revised specification of the post-March 1955 Transporter (the full list is lengthy, so only the most salient are itemised). Shortly, subtle improvements would be largely but not exclusively scooped together and presented at the beginning of each new model year, which from the summer of 1955 fell on 1 August each year:

- Cab floor inclined at the front.
- Foot recess for passenger.
- Sun visors for all models.
- Wing mirror mounted on door hinge.
- Cab seat repositioned higher – softer springing for comfort.
- Tailgate opened with a T handle.
- Engine compartment opened via a 'church' key.
- Doors with inside reinforcing plates.
- Nine outward facing air vents towards rear of vehicle on both sides (was eight).
- Reserve tap (no fuel gauge) relocated from engine bay to the cab.
- Reduction in the size of the wheels from 16 in. to 15 in.
- Beefier 6.40 x 15 tyres replacing skinny 5.50 x 16 tyres.
- Side loading door now has a handle with an integral lock.

3 April 1955 – One month to the day after the launch of the revised-look Transporter, owners in the USA, Canada and Guam no longer had to rely on the vagaries of semaphore indicators, instead sighing with relief as modern style flashing lamps were introduced, contained in what came to be referred to as 'bullet-style' housings. European market Transporters retained semaphores until the arrival of the '61 specification Transporters in the summer of 1960.

9 March 1956 – The first Transporter to roll off the assembly line in the new Hanover factory, a Pick-up finished in ubiquitous Dove Blue, was presented by factory manager Otto Höhne to the VW Distributor Dost of Hildesheim.

The Hop from Wolfsburg to Hanover

Few vehicles are granted their own factory within a few years of launch, but at face value that's exactly what happened to the Transporter. To make matters even more curious most will be aware that the onetime Nazi-owned factory at Wolfsburg was deliberately designed to be Europe's largest. Surely there must have been available space for Beetle and Transporter manufacture to sit side-by-side. The following extract from the 1958 brochure entitled, 'Getting ahead with Volkswagen Trucks and Station Wagons' spins the official line:

> The Volkswagen plant at Hanover – which went into production in 1956 – is considered to be the most modern and beautiful automobile factory in Europe ... This is a plant that was truly built by popular demand. Year after year, the great demand for Volkswagens required constantly increased production. It became imperative to build a new plant. Today the famous Wolfsburg plant produces sedans only. Over 2,000 roll off the assembly line each day. At Hanover, the daily production of trucks and station wagons exceeds 400.

The Hanover factory manager, Otto Höhne, presented the first Transporter to roll off the assembly line (a Pick-up) to the VW Distributor Dost of Hildesheim.

Sadly, for a book that eulogises the Transporter, the clue to the need for a new factory is contained within that single paragraph. The brochure copywriters proclaimed that in excess of 2,000 Beetles were produced every day. Nordhoff and his team simply couldn't keep up with demand. In 1955 well over a quarter of a million Beetles left Wolfsburg, an increase of 87,250 compared to the previous year. Nordhoff invested huge sums with the intention of creating sufficient supply to meet demand, but still there were ever-increasing waiting lists, a situation that would continue until the early 1960s. Capacity within Wolfsburg released to the Transporter would soon become an issue as the increase in volume between 1954 and 1955 (24 per cent), and 1955 and 1956 (25 per cent) serves to illustrate. Additionally, of the 35,000 residents of Wolfsburg, in excess of 24,000 worked at Volkswagen in one capacity or another. Put simply, VW were running out of staff. Amazingly, despite the 60-mile travelling distance between Hanover and Wolfsburg, reasonable numbers of workers commuted. The logical solution was to build a factory dedicated to the Transporter in Hanover, a city where there was a large and eager to work population to call on and leave Wolfsburg to concentrate on the Beetle.

The decision to go ahead was taken on 24 January 1955. On 4 February land at Stöcken on the outskirts of Hanover was officially acquired. Forty of the 112 hectares available were specifically allocated to assembly halls. Work started on 1 March; Nordhoff was in a hurry, but inevitably where he was concerned no corners were cut. The first vehicle to roll off the assembly line, a Pick-up painted in Dove Blue, did so on 8 March 1956, with full production following on 20 April. The original phase of the Hanover factory was fully completed by the summer of 1956. The western elevation and administration building extended some 378 m. Perhaps it doesn't come as a great surprise to discover that a second hall was under construction in 1958, while a further extension came to fruition in 1960. By 1962, 750 Transporters were being built daily as well as 5,000 engines. Needless to say, by this time the Hanover factory employed in excess of 20,000 people.

13 Sept 1956 – The 200,000th Transporter leaves Hanover.

1956 and an impressive shot of phase one of the all-new Hanover factory, built specifically to cater for mass production of the Transporter.

Right: Produced with a bang and a wallop – that's VW's 'at-a-slant' press photograph presentation, rather than the action of the Hanover body presses shown in the image.

Below: 'Surface treatment of bare body' is the caption produced for this Hanover factory assembly line press image.

Werkfoto
Works Photo
Photo VW

Volkswagenwerk - Werk Hannover
Karosserie-Pressen
Body presses
Presses de carrosserie

Abdruck honorarfrei
Reproduction allowed free of charge
Reproduction autorisée et gratuite

'Automatic spray priming of body' reads VW's caption for this Hanover Werks image.

A Favourite Across the World

Nordhoff had made it clear from the start. If Volkswagen was to be a multi-national success the US market had to be conquered. Here is not the place to recount the lengthy struggle undergone to entice the American purchaser to buy the Beetle in volume. Needless to say, though, where the Bug (as it was known in the USA) went the Transporter followed. Sadly, US sales of the Transporter in 1952 totalled less than ten; in 1953 the number was just thirty-three, to be followed in 1954 by a languid 271. Beetle sales were similarly disappointing but Nordhoff wasn't going to admit defeat. A further restructuring – or the selection of the right people for the task – worked. In 1955 as many as 2,021 Transporters were sold, while just three years later that number had been dwarfed with 25,268 sales being credited to Volkswagen's bank account. Numbers peaked in 1964, when a total of 40,198 Transporters were sold.

The British market, although by comparison to both the US and home markets sales were trivial, cannot be overlooked. In 1954, a year after Volkswagen Motors of Great Britain had been established, 827 Transporters were imported. By 1959 that figure had risen to a less than staggering 1,242. However, the advent of a new decade seems to have pulled the necessary trigger, with 3,029 examples making their way onto British roads in 1960. Like the US, sales of the first-generation Transporter peaked in 1964, when 3,800 sales were made.

While the vast majority of countries simply imported both Transporters and Beetles there were a few exceptions, the most significant of which was Brazil. 1953 saw the establishment of VW do Brasil SA, a body with a 20 per cent Brazilian shareholding, the remaining 80 per cent being held by Wolfsburg. The total number of Transporters, having been sold previously by the Chrysler Importer, was neither here nor there, and even under the auspices of the new company amounted to only forty-two examples in the year of its foundation. However, with a rented industrial unit at its disposal, the new company set about the business of assembling CKD (Completely Knocked Down) kits and although by the early part of 1957 only 552 vehicles had been sold, the vital step towards full manufacture had been taken. Undeterred by the lack of numbers, in 1956 work started on a 10,000 m² factory, approximately 14 miles from São Paulo, and it was here that Transporter manufacture started on 2 September 1957 – a full sixteen months ahead of the Beetle. Brazilian components initially extended to 50 per cent; by the end of the decade that had mushroomed to 95 per cent, in part a result of the success in terms of sales. 1958 had seen 4,819 Brazilian Transporters sold; by 1960 that had escalated to a rewarding 11,299, while a peak came the following year when 16,315 left the assembly line. Production hovered between a low of 12,000 and a high of over 15,000 vehicles in the years up to and including 1966. Production thereafter is covered in the final pages of this book.

Transporter imports to South Africa began in 1952 and by 1956 assembly was on the agenda. Demand for the Beetle was such that the Transporter always played second fiddle. Nevertheless, the urgency for both was sufficient that manufacture in addition to CKD, rather than as a replacement for it, was introduced, with investment in both press and engine machine shop. Gradually CKD kits were subjected to an increasing number of local components, while amazingly at the time, some Brazilian CKD kits were also imported. This was significant as it affected range options when production of the first-generation Transporter came to an end in Germany as will be seen at the end of the book.

The first year when Transporters were sold officially in Australia was 1953, although they debuted in the final months of the year. The year 1954 bore witness to 299 sales, a combination of fully assembled vehicles and CKD kits. In 1955 CKD assembly of the Transporter amounted to 546, only to be dwarfed the following year by a stunning increase to 2,989 vehicles. By 1960 this figure had grown to 3,944 Transporters and the prospect of full manufacture lay increasingly close by. A press shop was the first move and quick to follow were an engine manufacturing plant, a foundry and appropriately upgraded paint shop facilities. At the same time, local content of kit-built Transporters increased to 40 per cent, while gradually all models came to incorporate features unique to the market. Modifications prompted by Australia's arid and dusty climate (an example being the repositioning of the air intake vents from below to above the belt line) were probably most significant. However, in 1962, for the 1963 model year, Australia produced its own unique Container Van, a pastiche of the High Roof Delivery Van and a vehicle demanding the creation of a special body department. Slab sided, with doors of 63.5 in. in height and 42 in. in width, this was a vehicle worthy of special model status if it had been originated in Germany. Sadly, demand and attendant production of the first-generation Transporter dwindled noticeably as the 1960s passed their midway point, with just 1,568 examples being sold in 1966.

1 Nov 1957 – The 300,000th Transporter left Hanover. In 1957 demand for the Transporter, most notably the Micro Bus (Station Wagon), had grown to 19,000 units being exported to the USA.

29 Aug 1958 – US-bound models fitted with a new style of bumper with over-riders and a second 'rail' essentially to comply with legislation. However, the style proved very popular and many European customers paid extra to have them fitted.

01 Nov 1958 – Nordhoff's decision to move Transporter production from Wolfsburg to Hanover proved fully justified and he decided that the assembly of engines should also be transferred in order to release more workers and room to meet the insatiable demand for the Beetle.

19 May 1959 – Engine re-designed, although still 30 PS. This is typical of countless technical improvements which wouldn't attract the headlines but ensured ever-improving quality, longevity and resale values. As a characteristic example, in August of the same year, VW lengthened the gear and handbrake levers by 150 mm, and revised the pedal arrangements, while creating improved leg room in the cab.

25 Aug 1959 – Total Transporter production reached the magic half million mark.

Above, opposite and overleaf: Built on 29 February 1960, this superb and only lightly restored fifteen-window De Luxe is resplendent in numerous coats of Beige Grey (L472) over Sealing Wax Red (L53). From October 1958, all Transporters carried both a chassis plate and an 'M' plate (factory fitted options, or special equipment). This Model 241 Micro Bus Deluxe carries the M code 378, indicating a US specific package, equipment that consists of sealed beam headlamps, a laminated windscreen, US style bumpers (with the equivalent of towel rails), a speedometer calculated in mph and six pop-out side windows. M130 adds to the vehicle's rarity and is one of those unusual M codes which deletes, rather than adds, to the specification. Gone are the Samba's neat rows of roof-lights; gone too is the fold-back canvas sunroof, hence the moniker of fifteen-window. Photographed features include: the post-1955 dashboard common to all models, the Teutonic splendour of the vehicle's interior and quality personified, the bullet-shaped indicators current in the USA from 1955 to 1961, the trusty 30 PS engine and last, but not least, the vehicle's un-restored underneath which illustrates the nature of the longitudinal box sections and outriggers for support.

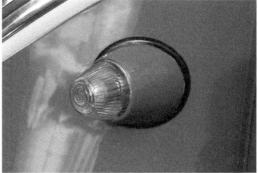

05 Jan 1960 – A day before his sixty-first birthday, Nordhoff addressed a large congregation of Transporter salesman preaching the success story that was the Delivery Van to the Micro Bus De Luxe.

No good reason exists why Transporter sales should be good in one country and disappointing in a neighbouring one. ... I repeat what I said two years ago, that the really big period for the Transporter hasn't even arrived yet. He who is clever will take his chances now. I have asked our sales department for years whether we shouldn't enlarge the capacity of our Hanover factory. I appreciate that I have been irritating about this, but I ask once more and with increasing urgency, for it takes at least two years to implement such a decision ... Now we produce 530 Transporters a day and I am certain that this isn't enough ... We need to move ahead ... we need to take what America calls a calculated risk...

Year-by-year growth in production and attendant sales of the Transporter vindicated Nordhoff's argument for expansion and would continue to do so for a few more years to come.

Transporter production numbers 1951–1964							
Year	Delivery Van	Micro Bus	Micro Bus De Luxe	Kombi	Pick-up	Ambulance	Total
1950	5,662	1,142		1,254			8,059
1951	6,049	2,805	269	2,843	1	36	12,003 (48.9% increase on 1950)
1952	9,353	4,052	1,142	5,031	1,606	481	21,665 (80.1% increase)
1953	11,190	4,086	1,289	5,753	5,741	358	28,417 (31.1% increase)
1954	14,550	5,693	1,937	8,868	8,562	589	40,119 (41.2% increase)
1955	17,577	7,957	2,195	11,346	10,138	694	49,907 (24.4% increase)
1956	22,357	9,726	2,072	16,010	11,449	586	62,500 (25% increase on 1955)
1957	30,683	17,917	3,514	23,495	16,450	644	91,983 (47% increase)
Although the Transporter had been sold in an increasing number of countries, until 1957 no operations, other than Wolfsburg and later Hanover, were involved in the manufacture of Transporters for their own market. Foremost amongst those assembling Transporters and manufacturing Transporters were Volkswagen do Brasil. Worldwide production numbers are shown in brackets below each year heading.							
1958 (105,562)	36,672	19,499	4,342	21,732	19,142	486	101,873 (11% increase)
1959 (129,836)	41,395	22,934	6,241	25,699	24,465	710	121,453 (19% increase)
1960 (151,218)	47,498	22,504	7,846	30,425	30,988	658	139,919 (15% increase)

1961 (168,600)	45,121	25,410	8,095	25,950	36,822	883 +4	152,285 (9% increase)
1962 (127,324)	47,237	29,898	11,280	38,506	38,118	728	165,774 (9% increase)
1963 (189,294)	47,891	31,196	14,764	40,882	39,458	675	174,866 (5.5% increase)
1964 (200,325)	48,481	40,115	14,031	44,659	39,832	829	187,947 (7.5% increase)

Three Initials Spell Success

As the 1950s were approaching an end, concern was mounting in the USA amongst the big Detroit car manufacturers – Ford, General Motors and Chrysler – that ever-increasing sales of the Beetle were set to endanger their stranglehold on the US market. Their answer was to contemplate similarly sized cars of their own. Reacting to this news, Volkswagen's head of American operations, Carl Hahn, a future Director General of Volkswagen and a protégé of Nordhoff's, decided he needed to market the Beetle in a more aggressive manner than simple word of mouth. After considerable deliberation he appointed the relatively recently formed ad agency of Doyle Dane Bernbach (DDB) to produce a series of adverts designed to maintain, or further improve, the current numbers in the face of a new challenge. DDB broke the mould. Stark single theme and honest photography was matched by crisp one message, one advert text. Humour, self-deprecating messages and a clean uncluttered storyline was unheard of in automobile advertising and proved an instant success. Beetle sales didn't falter, but instead grew, the car acquiring cult status.

For the Transporter, Hahn decided initially to award the advertising account to an established agency, Fuller and Smith and Ross. Twelve months later he invested his entire budget in DDB. Transporter sales in the USA grew accordingly as such headlines as, 'We also make a funny looking car' (picture of Micro Bus De Luxe), 'That's about the size of it' (Beetle outline painted on Transporter body showing the latter to be only a little longer) and 'Somebody actually stole one', caught the public's imagination.

1 June 1960 – New 34 PS engine with a compression ratio of 7.0:1 (previously 6.6:1) and an automatic choke.

1 June 1960 – European market Transporters now fitted with flashing bullet-shaped indicators.

31 July 1961 – US market Transporters fitted with larger 'fish-eye' style front indicators. New two-section rear lights (one amber for indicators, except US where both sections are red).

31 July 1961 – Fuel gauge fitted to all models.

30 July 1962 – Divided seat (one plus two) replaces bench seat. Driver's seat adjustable.

20 Sept 1962 – The millionth Transporter leaves the Hanover assembly line.

The Numbers Game

Reference has already been made to the successive arrivals of the 100,000th, then the 200,000th and, at the time, the landmark 500,000th Transporter. All paled into insignificance in comparison to the event that occurred on 20 September 1962, when the millionth Transporter, a suitably garlanded Micro Bus De Luxe, as befitted the occasion, was paraded to the press and dealers alike.

Nordhoff was inevitably on hand and made his customary lengthy speech to mark the occasion. The significance of the content, particularly how Nordhoff and the automotive world saw the Transporter, warrants reproduction of several paragraphs from it.

> In November 1949 I asked the representatives of the Press to Wolfsburg, to attend the unveiling of the VW Transporter. In those early days our daily production amounted to some 200 vehicles and we were very proud of that. In those days the VW Transporter was something completely new and original.
>
> No-one foresaw that it would become the forerunner to a completely new type of vehicle, representing as it did an often near-slavishly copied genre of utility vehicles.

The garland-bedecked millionth Transporter, a Micro Bus De Luxe, which rolled off the Hanover assembly line on 20 September 1962.

When one mentions vehicles, one usually thinks of cars, but production of these small Transporters, up to 1,000 kg, represents a considerable industry in its own right, probably the newest in the entire automobile industry, both in Europe and the USA.

Although it also includes the manufacture of engines, it was thanks to the Transporter that we began to build our factory in Hanover, which now employs 20,000 people. 63 per cent of all Transporters are exported, and their market share in this newly created sector is very high in many countries. It is 40.5 per cent in this country, but in Belgium, Holland, Austria, Sweden and Switzerland it is 50 per cent or more. Even in the United States it stands at five per cent, which is in fact a great achievement, taking into account the size of the US market. The VW Transporter is not only the original, but also remains the leader in this class.

In the relatively short time of less than fifteen years, something completely new has been created by the VW Factory, of which it can be said "Often copied, never equalled".

Since that November of 1949 a million of these VW Transporters have been bought and sold, and even if we are now used to this million phenomenon, it seems to us to be an achievement of such fundamental importance, that we have asked you to come again and celebrate this festive and meaningful day with us; to view the rapid development of our factories and to chat with us about the never-ending subject of automobiles.

10 Oct 1962 – Air heated in heat exchangers rather than by cylinders; decreases risk of fumes.

7 Jan 1963 – New 1,500 cc engine (initially only for US market). Increased bore and stroke of 83 mm x 69 mm, compression ratio 7.5:1. 1,493 cc engine offers 42 PS at 3,800 rpm. Top speed recommended of 65 mph. Transporter payload increased as a result from 750 kg to 1,000 kg. Nordhoff was so concerned that owners would ignore factory advice regarding speed that, with effect from August 1964, a governor was fitted to the carburettor.

5 Aug 1963 – Tailgate enlarged and larger rear window. The Micro Bus De Luxe loses its curved rear pillar windows.

5 Aug 1963 – Larger 'fish-eye' indicator lens replaces bullet-style flasher on European market models.

19 Dec 1963 – 14 in. wheels replace 15 in. ones.

2 Aug 1965 – 1500 engine fitted with larger valves to improve breathing. Power increases from 42 PS to 44 PS at 4,000 rpm.

1 Aug 1966 – 12-volt electrics standard (previously optional) replacing the reliance on 6 volts, regarded by most as antiquated then and bordering on irresponsible in later years.

July 1967/1 Aug 1967 – The last first-generation Transporter left the assembly line towards the end of July 1967, immediately before the annual factory shutdown and holidays. When the workforce returned at the beginning of August their endeavours were concentrated on building a new type of Transporter with many features which brought it up to date. The antiquated split-screen windscreen was probably the most noticeable feature to go, its place being taken by a panoramic single piece of glass, which earned the second-generation Transporter the nickname 'Bay'.

Above: In this charming publicity shot, the millionth Transporter leads the way as ranks of varying models leave the factory to be shepherded onto waiting railway transportation trucks.

Left: What variety – the cover of an untitled brochure dating from 1964, which serves to illustrate the wide variety of models available as standard.

The larger tailgate and hatch window were introduced on 5 August 1963 for the 1964 model year and at the expense of the Samba's rear corner glasses. Overnight a twenty-three-window model became a twenty-one-window Micro Bus De Luxe.

This well-used and loved late model Transporter features the large indicator housings, known as fish-eyes in enthusiast circles, which were introduced in 1961 in the USA and 1963 for European markets and beyond.

The End Game

Nordhoff's detractors frequently declared in the last years of his life that the Director General was incapable of changing model, of clinging to the past. Nothing could have been further from the truth in the case of the Transporter.

Amazingly, a potential replacement for the first-generation Transporter emerged in prototype form, and under the code name EA114, as early as 1960. Admittedly its rejection was swift, but Nordhoff didn't close the door to other development projects completely. Four years later in 1964, the Volkswagen board, under Nordhoff's leadership, directed Gustav Mayer, head of the design and development department for commercial vehicles, to start in earnest on the creation of a worthy successor to the then fifteen/fourteen-year-old model. In typical Nordhoff style Mayer was set a series of deadlines which would ensure the programme did not extend over three years. In 1966 the first prototypes were ready to undergo serious road testing.

Whether Nordhoff was such a master of his craft that he could predict the downturn in Transporter sales in 1965, following the record of 187,947 set in the previous year, cannot be quantified. However, by the time of the arrival of the second-generation Transporter in August 1967, it was clear that, despite a period of economic depression which affected Germany (and many other countries too) for the first time since its regeneration after the war, sales were dwindling. Dealers and individual customers alike welcomed the arrival of the thoroughly modern, panoramic windscreen model.

Transporter production numbers: the final years, 1965–67							
1965 (189,876)	43,723		37,933	12,467	44,331	37,444	864	176,762 (−6%)
1966 (191,373)	43,084		30,767	18,790	46,284	36,534	816	176,275
1967 (162,741)	Figures cannot be broken down – includes second generation Transporter							141,569

A Multiplicity of Special Models and the Campervan

Few, other than Nordhoff and the chosen few who were privy to his innermost thoughts, realised the Transporter's potential when the prototypes were lined up for the world's automotive press to prod and poke in November 1949, or when the first examples rolled off the Wolfsburg assembly line a few months later. While model diversity was illustrated by the presence of a vehicle other than a Delivery Van at the press launch and it was apparent that both the Kombi and Micro Bus were not far behind Wolfsburg's first option when production started, even the most experienced automotive hack failed to realise the potential for near infinite diversity.

House Colours, Logos and Product Advertising

A clue was presented in the first vehicle to leave Wolfsburg as part of the official production run. Not only was this Delivery Van presented to the purchasing dealer in nothing more than its primer underclothes, it also lacked the soon to be traditional

The first official Transporter sale was of this Delivery Van which was delivered in primer to Autohaus Fleischhauer for the 4711 perfume company. The van was painted in the company's house colours and its logo replaced the VW roundel on the front panel.

VW roundel on its front panel. This was to be a Delivery Van presented in the house colours of its new owners and appropriately logoed. A hint of such usage had been apparent with one of the prototypes, which carried extravagant three-dimensional lettering proclaiming it to be, no doubt wishfully, the 'property' of the 'Wolfsburger Delikatessen'.

A reasonable number of would-be owners clearly saw the advantages of buying a Transporter finished in primer, as official figures reveal. For the home market in 1950, 2,356 Delivery Vans left Wolfsburg fully painted, but a quite amazing 1,989 examples departed with bare metal only protected by primer. Kombi figures offer 919 in gloss compared to 264 in primer, while with the more upmarket Micro Bus, which obviously attracted business owners as well as being a family 'saloon', 780 had a gloss finish

A Micro Bus for the Swedish market. This cover image of an eight-page brochure, which dates from 1952, reveals a colour scheme which wasn't a part of VW's in-house palette. Think primer and the adoption of 'house' colours.

Note the three-dimensional lettering on the side of this sign-written Delivery Van, a feature reminiscent of a Wolfsburg prototype of 1949 vintage.

and 145 went away from Wolfsburg in primer. Across the three models, a further 543 Transporters were exported wearing primer. Hopefully, few had to make their inaugural journeys by sea.

Such was the appeal of the paint-your-own Transporters that in 1951 the marketing people organised a twenty-four-page brochure dedicated to nothing more than straightforward black and white imagery of eighty-one sign-written vehicles, mostly, but not exclusively, Delivery Vans. As a bonus, the inside front cover was devoted to a colour image of the father of them all, the first production model, painted in the house colours of the 4711 perfume company and complete with a chromed front bumper, whilst carrying a logoed front panel in place of the missing VW roundel. The inside back cover was similarly presented in colour, this time dedicated to a rear shot of a logoed red Delivery Van, while the outside back cover was allocated to a delightful sign-written van, the property of a toyshop and complete with an image of a toy soldier riding a white rocking horse.

1952 saw the brochure reissued but in a much more elaborate fifty-four-page format, complete with both an occasional daub of colour throughout and subtle backgrounds which associated the trade or profession of the company or owner of the pictured Transporter to the vehicle itself. Micro Buses painted in the house colours of various airlines were linked to greyscale imagery of the latest long or short-haul aeroplanes, Delivery Vans owned by suppliers of typewriters were associated with abstract drawings of individual keys, while newspaper Delivery Vans, or even Kombis, numerous in number, were represented either against both a background of newspaper titles, each in their own distinctive script, or a wallpaper of column inches interspersed with headings such as 'London answers Persian protest'.

Similarly themed sales literature would emerge again in a comparatively short space of time, by which time the theme had been extended to incorporate not just sign-writing and house colours, but also interiors where adaptations had been made suited to the trade or profession of the particular Transporter's owners. However, before turning to such extravagances, Nordhoff had another way of offering the customers what they wanted.

A June 1960 Signal Red, sign-written, double-door Delivery Van, which illustrates the ongoing popularity of making full use of what Volkswagen described as a 'large advertising space'. Note the unusual 'skylight' above the cab window.

Above: A particularly attractive Pick-up advertises a very well-known brand of petroleum!

Left: Repainted! Built on 26 January 1951, for the past thirty years and more this Kombi has been used at a gliding school near Stuttgart. Although the livery is reminiscent of Lufthansa, the cab doors carry the logo of the gliding school.

Special Equipment (*Mehrausstattung*)

The November 1950 edition of the in-house magazine entitled *VW Information* introduced the concept of special equipment specific to an individual customer's needs. Items under discussion included roof racks and extensions, while the vital statistics of the Delivery Van's interior were accompanied by line drawings for those contemplating fitting anything from shelves to internal cladding. Most significantly of all, details were given of how a dealership, for example, could either fit a rear window, or go much further and create an opening rear hatch.

From such small beginnings there developed a lengthy series of special equipment codes ('M' codes), many of which added to the specification of an individual Transporter. However, options specific to a given market, involving both additions to and deletions from the standard specification, as well as general options to simplify the normal presentation, were also included. 'M' codes were set to play an important part in the specification of the range of Transporters throughout the seventeen-year history of the first-generation Transporter and beyond. The numbers allocated, however, did not necessarily remain constant as, for example, when an 'M' option became part of a standard specification, it might well have been reissued to another potential enhancement or deletion.

The list of 'M' codes is extensive. Examples of the most popular and obscure, those specific to a given market and ones relating to deletions, are all included in the following summary list:

M004 dust free air intake (Pick-up); M023 LHD Delivery Van with side-loading doors on left; M025 six pop-out windows and US bumpers; M027 windscreen washer (Australian market only); M028 Ambulance without stretcher; M030 Delivery Van or Kombi in primer; M040 speedometer with fuel gauge; M055 tailgate with window (until March 1955);

A page from the 1952, lavish sixty-four-page brochure entitled, *Wer Fahrt VW Transporter* ('Who drives the VW Transporter'), which offered pictures of a near inexhaustible list of specialist use Transporters. Created a few years before the emergence of official SO designations, here we have a very early interpretation of a Transporter adapted for use as a mobile shop.

Here's what was essentially an Ambulance originally, which has been adapted to house an easily removable life support pod.

M066 rubber mat for load area; M080 walk-through cab for LHD Delivery Van and Kombi; M091 whitewall tyres; M093 Behr air scoop (until March 1955); M097 rear bumper (until March 1955); M113 safari windows (export models); M118 Pick-up minus side gates; M119 Eberspächer auxiliary heater for all standard models excepting the Pick-up; M127 tailgate without a window; M173 engine prepared for arctic conditions (extra heavy duty insulation of the engine compartment); M181 chrome hubcaps; M192 body ready to be fitted as a camper; M200 Pick-up with extended steel platform; M201 Pick-up with extended wooden platform; M211 seating for nine people with sliding doors both sides; M221 High Roof Delivery Van with sales flap; M225 VW Dealer Breakdown/Service vehicle; M303 complies with Italian market regulations; M396 complies with British market (amber indicator sections, right-hand-drive); M415, extended long load bed for the Pick-up; M502 board side panelling for Delivery Van or Kombi; M520 sliding doors left and right; M529 cab partition with sliding window; M620 12-volt electrical system (standard from August 1966).

Special Models (*Sonderausführungen*)

If the initial use of 'M' codes was in most instances a way of tailoring a Transporter to an individual customer's needs, a more-or-less parallel and steadily growing series of options offered the same but on a much grander scale. The February/March 1951 issue of *VW Information* carried details, sketches and even pictures of a variety of Transporters which had been adapted to suit customer needs if not by the dealership, then by a coachbuilding firm on its behalf. Reference has already been made to the forerunner of Volkswagen's in-house Ambulance, the work of the coachbuilder Meisen and to the firm Binz of Lorch Württemberg, who created a double cab version of the Pick-up in 1953 and whose idea would be annexed by VW a few years later.

In 1955, Volkswagen's marketing department collated the many models produced by a wide variety of coachbuilders into a multi-lingual, but largely pictorial, brochure entitled (in English) 'Interior Equipment for Volkswagen Transporters'. The result was an impressive fifty-page piece of print depicting all manner of models, each placed with others of a similar ilk, the carefully constructed single colour backgrounds highlighting the profession or trade the special had been built for. Flicking through the pages, the eye variously rests on a fully shelved cargo area of a Delivery Van, a mobile shop (complete with awning), an assortment of Pick-ups, Delivery Vans and Kombis dispensing beverages ranging from Coca Cola to potent alcohol, Transporters adapted for the carrying of livestock (the attendant imagery shows pigs and piglets), police mobile communication centres (complete with klaxon, decidedly un-portable phones and even a typewriter), a life support pod vehicle of apparent immense sophistication, a mobile library overflowing with books featuring lurid cover imagery, a sheet of glass carrying Pick-up and, most interesting of all, a series of Transporters used for camping purposes.

The following year, 1956 saw the first official designations allocated to conversions, with the implication that only those not built at Wolfsburg or Hanover were included in any published listing. To compound each *sonderaufbauten* (literally 'special structure') the town or city from which the coachbuilder operated was included in the designation. To make matters easy for future generations, the dealer Mahag of Munich included a four-page leaflet of special models with a set of main model brochures, the whole package being contained within a heavy-duty folder. Each of the following models was illustrated and, as will be seen, most, but not all, included both a SO designation and 'location':

Pick-up with wooden platform, Type Munich, made of tongue and groove boards; Pick-up with wooden platform, Type SO9 Wiedenbrück, made of plywood; VW Pick-up with widened all-steel body Type SO8 Marburg; VW Pick-up with light metal blinds, Type SO12 Minden; VW Pick-up with aerial ladder, Type SO11; VW mobile shop, Type SO1 Wiedenbrück; VW Pick-up with double cabin, Type SO16 Lorch; VW Pick-up with box body, Type SO13 Wiedenbrück; VW Transporter as a refrigerated or insulated vehicle, Type Munich; Cooling compartment, Type Munich, for installation in the VW Delivery Van or in the Kombi; VW Transporter as a fire brigade and fire truck, type TSF-T (VW Delivery Van with fire equipment to German standards M140 and heating vents in the load area 141); VW Transporter, as ambulance, Type 271, livery Ivory White or RAL Grey; VW Transporter, as a workshop car, Type SO18 Frankfurt; VW Transporter with camping facility, Type SO22 Wiedenbrück and De Luxe Type SO23 – Delivery Van, VW Kombi, Eight-seater and Special Model (Micro Bus De Luxe); Traffic Accident vehicle, Type SO4 Wiedenbrück; Traffic Accident VW Kombi without 'loading area' seats, Police Green; VW Pick-up carrying long goods and general cargo trailer, Type SO24 Neuenhaus, Type SO14 Winsen; VW Delivery Van with WIDO installation shelves.

VW-Verkaufswagen (SO 1)

By 1958 Volkswagen were producing a first series of double-sided single sheets, promoting individual recognised special models. The mobile shop version shown here bore the accolade of SO1.

From late 1957 the first official listing of the special models proving to be most popular became available from any dealership. As with the 1955 brochure, which included unallocated imagery of Transporters converted for camping usage, and the Mahag publication, which made specific reference to Westfalia products, the new definitive listing included the designations SO22 and SO23, a style by which subsequent models of Camper would be known to this day. The list ran as follows:

SO1 Mobile Shop, SO3/4 Police Accident and Command vehicles, SO5 Insulated Cold Transport Van with both dry-ice fan blower and 140 mm insulating board, SO6 Insulated Cold Transport Van with 80 mm insulating board, SO7 Refrigerated, SO8 Pick-up with wide metal loading platform, SO9 Pick-up with wide wooden loading platform, SO11 Pick-up Ladder Truck, SO12 Pick up Box style van with Aluminium roller shutter doors, SO13 Pick-up with enclosed storage box, SO14 Pole-carrying trailer (no storage, wheeled unit only) and mounting for platform, SO15 Pick-up with hydraulic platform tipper, SO16 Binz Double Cab, SO18 Mobile Workshop/Breakdown Vehicle, SO19 Display/Exhibition vehicle, SO21 Wido Multi-layout shelving, SO22 Westfalia Camping Box, SO23 Westfalia De Luxe Camper, SO24 Trailer with storage facilities and mounting for Pick-up platform for the transportation of long poles or pipes, SO29 Red Cross emergency/disaster Trailer unit, SO30 Drag Sled stretcher for use in the mines, SO32 Pick-up Enclosed Box Van (variant on SO12)

Now established, the SO models could be ordered at any VW dealership in Germany and beyond, but all were approved by Volkswagen's development department, maintaining the high standard required and as a result, carrying a full ex-works warranty. Many incorporated at least a smattering of 'optional' VW authorised, or developed, factory-fitted components.

Behind the side doors, the storage compartment is accessible through a refrigerator-type door. The door fittings are chromium-plated against corrosion.

When the doors are open an easily removable apron prevents the cold air from escaping.

VW Refrigerator Van with compressor type refrigerator unit

The first rule of the road for vans carrying frozen food — or indeed fruit, vegetables, fish, meat, or perishables of any kind, is "keep cool" — and the second is "keep moving — fast".

Being in the food business you know the importance of having a reliable transportation link all the way — from the packers to the wholesalers, the wholesalers to the retailers and from there to the customer's home.

Once again you will find that Volkswagen has designed just the van you need. Make sure your perishable foods — frozen or chilled — reach your customers in first class condition — in a VW Refrigerator Van.

The wooden slats protect the floor of the storage compartment.

Above and below: By 1960 English language versions of the leaflets promoting given special models were available. Although no reference is made to its SO designation of 7, the refrigerated freezer van (this is indeed what it is) was a vehicle often used by the Blood Transfusion Service.

The selection switches and pilot lamps of the drive units are installed within the direct range of the driver.

The refrigeration unit is conveniently housed in the space above the vehicle engine — easily accessible through the rear lid of the VW Van.

The storage compartment is fully insulated. The insulation material (Silian felt and Expansit) is embedded in an impregnated light wood structure. A particularly efficient and by the same token very economic cooling is obtained through this novel construction. Aluminium pipes acting as evaporators are run within the Expansit material. Furthermore, the inside of the insulating layer is clad with aluminium foil. Thanks to this practical arrangement the cooling system possesses a very extensive surface. Each part of the storage compartment is evenly and thoroughly cooled.

On the side of the storage compartment the insulating material together with the pipes is covered with aluminium sheet. All joints are specially protected by aluminium slats. Any ingress of moisture into the insulation is prevented — the evaporator pipes do not become frosted — no defrosting system is required. No metal contact exists between inner lining and outer panel of the vehicle, thus avoiding any cold exchange to the outside.

The refrigeration unit comprises a piston compressor with two cylinders, a coolant receiver and the drive units. It is powered by the vehicle's engine — when running — or, for stationary operation, by a built-in electric motor which can be plugged to the local power system.

Provision has been made for the safe and convenient operation of the refrigeration unit. The temperature is thermostat-controlled. A remote thermometer in the driver's cabin offers an additional control feature.

A conclusive example of the quality and reliability of the equipment: Even at a temperature of + 50° C (+ 123° F) a constant temperature of − 20° C (− 5° F) can be maintained in the storage compartment.

VOLKSWAGENWERK GMBH · WOLFSBURG

A removable aluminium tube shelf, which can be supplied as an extra, offers additional storage space.

77

The Binz Double Cab Pick-up was given the SO designation of 17. Note the rather obvious cut down nature of the side gate on view and an odd, amateurish panel configuration where additions have been made to the original single cab. Despite VW being eager to adopt the Double Cab as a core model made at Hanover, it is presumed that Binz sold no more than 550 of their allegedly popular conversion.

By 1958, Volkswagen had introduced single leaf sales brochures specific to given SO designations and continued to issue updates on these, as well as more elaborate material for certain categories of special models, such as fire and police vehicles.

By the advent of the 1960s, Volkswagen could present a lengthy list of 130 approved special models. The marketing department opted to capitalise on such a number, returning to the production of a further multi-lingual but slimmer, and still largely photographic, thirty-two-page brochure, neatly entitled 'VW Commercials equipped for many purposes'. Although the VW Camper was notable by its absence, with more mundane models covering most of the pages, two concise paragraphs of text on the brochure's back cover present a perfect résumé of why Transporter sales escalated year-on-year.

> Some special bodies and special equipment would either be too expensive for the individual buyers to fit, or else special safety regulations would prevent him from doing this ... Therefore, the Volkswagen factory also offers you a range of special models which are in series production. These vehicles which have been developed and tested in close collaboration with people who use them, have already proved their worth many times over.
>
> Your Volkswagen dealer has got a full range of literature giving details of these models just waiting there for you. Pay him a visit.

In trades where versatility is given top priority
the VW Pick-up with a double cabin really fills the
bill. Goods, people or both—whatever your
transport problem, this VW Pick-up will solve it
without hesitation. You can carry all sorts of
freight in an enclosed compartment, on an open
platform or under bows and tarpaulin—and all
with one and the same vehicle!

THE VW PICK-UP WITH DOUBLE CABIN

— a versatile vehicle
suitable for many trades

When is a core model not an integral part of the main VW range? Answer: when it appears with its own double-sided brochure the year following its launch!

Although this Ladder Truck was converted by the French firm of Echelles Vadot, its similarity to the SO11 (converted by Bischoff and Hamel in Germany) is noticeable.

This High Roof SO1 (mobile shop) dates from 1964 and belonged to Coca Cola for many a year.

It would easily be possible for someone to write a book about VW's offerings appropriate to the fire services and police.

This fire Bus was converted in 1957. The indicator pods below the windscreen are a later addition. The vehicle was originally a Delivery Van, but windows have been added.

A notable blurring of the divisions between core and special models became apparent when later sales literature depicted a selection of vehicles with SO designations but included in their midst Transporters such as the High Roof Delivery Van and the Ambulance. Perhaps the Micro Bus De Luxe had been referred to as a special model many moons earlier, but surely it was inappropriate to line it up alongside the likes of a freezer van and a Pick-up with hydraulic lifting platform.

Westfalia Campers

To the average person today, and possibly even a percentage of VW enthusiasts, the term VW Camper embraces all models, presumably because the majority of survivors from the earlier generations of Transporters are indeed campers or started life as Delivery Vans, Kombis and Micro Buses and have subsequently been converted for recreational usage.

While modern day Volkswagen has built its own campers, branded the California, since the debut of the fifth-generation Transporter in 2003, it is important to reiterate that Wolfsburg and Hanover were not involved in the production of a camper for any of their numerous markets. In Germany, from the loosest of informal arrangements with the coachbuilder Westfalia, a relationship gradually developed whereby an interior installed in either a Kombi or Micro Bus, built especially for the occasion, first warranted a SO number and, later in the 1950s, appropriately glossy brochures. Far removed from those produced for other special models and dedicated to the Camper alone, these were the province of Volkswagen's marketing department. Westfalia, for their part, opened a dedicated Camper assembly line in 1958.

Nordhoff had recognised that, ultimately, success was only possible for Volkswagen if they were able to conquer at least a segment of the US market. As the 1950s gave way to the new decade that goal was at least partially achieved, but there was an issue as far as the Transporter was concerned. Americans desired the Camper much more than they wanted Delivery Vans, Kombis and even Pick-ups. Almost 75 per cent of Westfalia's output was destined for export, the US accounting for much of the 30,000-vehicle total announced in 1968. Such was the demand in the USA that dealers there turned to local businesses to build what in essence were replica Westfalia models. Unfortunately, or fortunately for them, the poor turnover of Delivery Vans and their like and VWoA's insistence on a take it or leave it arrangement, whereby dealers had to buy these slow movers or they didn't qualify for a quota of Campers, gave them a decent supply of VWs as host vehicles. Such was the similarity of the Campers built by the likes of Sportsmobile (founded in Texas in 1961) that, amongst certain enthusiasts, such Campmobiles (a term devised by the advertising agency DDB and readily adopted by VWoA) are jokingly known as *Westfakias*.

The inability of Westfalia to meet US demand had consequences elsewhere. While the home market was served reasonably well, even including options more favourable to Europe than the US, no attempt was made to produce RHD conversions for the British market. This left the door wide open for fledgling UK operations to produce Campers, with one, J. P. White of Sidmouth in Devon, striking a deal with VW's British concession to become the licensed or recommended Camper agency through Volkswagen's network of distributors and dealers.

Above, below and opposite: One of several US-produced camper conversions designed to fill the hole left by Westfalia's inability to meet demand. Most, as this one does, made use of a Delivery Van as the host, as illustrated by the rather obvious smaller side windows carved out of the long side panel. A quick glance at the interior shows how close to the real thing the work of Riviera (which this isn't), Sundial (which it is) and others were to Westfalia's craftsmanship and design, making each worthy of a place in VW of America's showrooms.

Origins of Westfalia's Success

Franz Knöbel & Söhne KG, the name behind the Westfalia-Werke, has origins which stem back to 1844. The company was, for many years, highly successful, changing with the times and surviving both the First and Second World War and the attendant depression following the cessation of the former. Progress after 1945, despite a badly bombed factory, was remarkable, producing trailers and to a certain extent caravans, ensuring that 300 employees were on the payroll by the end of 1950. As such, any thoughts of work on the Transporter were peripheral to the company's main target markets, despite the opportunity of creating a removable interior for a market probably not yet exploited.

Although the occasional jaundiced individual has suggested that the legend of how Westfalia's first VW Camper came to be built is no more than that, most accept the story as accurate. Separate to random thoughts concerning what would become known as the Camping Box for use in conjunction with the multi-purpose Kombi, a US officer serving in Germany approached Westfalia with a request to build a one-off caravan-style interior for his VW. Having successfully completed this task, Westfalia carefully handcrafted a further fifty Camper vans during the course of 1952 and entered into brief discussions with Volkswagen and displayed what was regarded as a prototype at the Frankfurt Motor Show in the same year.

Alongside the fully fledged Camper, Westfalia designed furniture that could be taken out of a hard-working Kombi during the week. A non-too-literal translation of a key paragraph of the first Westfalia brochure dedicated to the VW Transporter, and dated 1953, illustrates beautifully what was a brilliant concept in the 1950s, but out of the question today!

> Isn't the versatility behind the make-up of the Westfalia Camping Box truly amazing? Because it is easy and convenient to install into the vehicle you use during the week, you are adding a new dimension to the use of your Transporter. But it isn't just with the VW Kombi that you have more versatility than ever before. Suppose you have visitors who want to stay overnight, then … you bring some of the Camping Kit inside your house and the problem is solved. The same applies if you choose to camp out in a hunting lodge or a boathouse. We wish you a happy start to your summer excursions and weekend breaks, which you can now plan while knowing that you are saving significant amounts of money too.

Reference has already been made to the first SO numbers allocated to the Westfalia Camping Box (SO22) and its De Luxe sibling, the fully fitted out SO23. Before that the company had published a brochure entitled 'Westfalia presents the holiday home on wheels', a six-page colour offering to market the new-for-1956 'Volkswagen Kombi with Westfalia de Luxe Camping Equipment' model.

Ihr Landhaus auf Rädern!

Dating from 1953, this brochure produced by Westfalia was designed to promote the Camping Box, a glimpse of the case of which can be seen to the right of the image. The brochure is entitled, 'Your country house on wheels'.

Direct from Westfalia, this image of pre-1958 vintage portrays their 'holiday home on wheels', or their first De Luxe Camping Equipment model.

The SO23 replaced this conversion in late 1958, lasting until April 1961, when it too was replaced by the SO34 and SO35. The SO23 is often regarded as defining and came complete with what became Westfalia's archetypal plaid upholstery, a wardrobe with a delightful rounded dressing mirror on its door, a convenient child-friendly bunk bed in the cab, a well-appointed layout that included dining and seating facilities, plus a toiletry/washing/kitchen area, a submarine type fresh-air hatch and, as a pièce de résistance, the luxury of ten variously coloured metal beakers fitted within a Plexiglas container.

The most significant difference between the SO23 and its successors, the SO34 and 35, apart from the choice of two finishes, white and grey laminate or dark Swiss pear wood and varying upholsteries, was an ingenious flip-seat arrangement. In other words, the cab seat backrest could be flipped when the Camper was not in motion, this device affording far more room in the living area than would have been the case if a separate purpose-built bench had been inserted.

1965 saw the introduction of two new models, conversions which would prove to be the last applicable to the first-generation Transporter. Most notably, the SO42 retained the traditional layout pattern that appealed to so many and particularly to US residents. The second model, designated the SO44, was essentially a European-market-only bulkhead model, a layout which saw a substantial wardrobe placed behind the driver's seat, abutted to which was the equivalent of a dominant kitchen layout incorporating a sink, ample storage and what could be loosely termed as a refrigerator.

The easiest way to distinguish between the SO42 and earlier Westfalia incarnations is to glance at the roof – gone was the submarine style roof hatch. In its place there was a small ventilation orientated pop-top, a feature which was set to survive into the era of the second-generation Transporter.

THE VOLKSWAGEN CAMPER

WITH WESTFALIA DE LUXE EQUIPMENT

Above and below: Two lovely cover images produced for successive year brochures handed out by Volkswagen to proclaim the story and assets of the SO23 (1958–1962).

THE VOLKSWAGEN CAMPER

WITH WESTFALIA DE LUXE EQUIPMENT

Useful »Extras« for all VW Camping Car models:

Large side tent
with attachable toilet compartment
Chemical toilet
(»Elsan Blue« chemicals)
Sun roof accessories for large side tent
Small side tent

Canvas cover for roof rack
Curtain with rod
between driver's cab and living room
Eberspächer stationary heater
with extended heating tube
Coleman petrol cooker

As the words accompanying the image indicate, customers could buy individual units to create their own camping car.

Here's the SO34 of late 1961 to 1965 vintage. Different to, rather than better than, the SO23 it succeeded, the latest offering from Westfalia featured white and grey laminates, a delightful cab seat that flipped and became part of the camping area and variations on Westfalia's famous plaid seat coverings.

VW Camping Car

Above, below and opposite: The SO44, 1965–1967, is something of a rarity as it was much less popular than its sibling, the SO42. Unlike previous Westfalia conversions, this was a fully fledged bulkhead offering with a tall, large wardrobe behind the driver and a kitchen unit with both sink and tap, filling the remaining space. A new pull-out style of bed and a pop-up elevating roof (which replaced the equivalent of a submarine hatch) were offered with both the SO44 and 42.

The Devon Camper

Although J. P. White's Devon operation was quickly granted 'official' status, it should not be assumed that its status bore a close resemblance to that of Westfalia. While the German company faced challenges from a number of competitors at home, it had the prestige of official SO designations. Devon, on the other hand, hadn't and never would. A whole gamut of other conversion companies, from the likes of early players linked to VW dealers, to later interventions from a big name like Dormobile, or the highly competitive fledgling

Danbury operation, always posed a potential threat. Indeed, post the first-generation era both aforementioned names were granted Volkswagen approved status alongside Devon, but that's a tale for another volume of the VW Transporter story.

Successful Sidmouth-based builder Jack White had sold his Beetle in favour of a Transporter, his family having outgrown the capacity of the car. During the winter months of 1955 into 1956 and with the help of his master craftsman designer of kitchen units, Pat Mitchell, Jack created a camping interior with passenger comforts for his Delivery Van. The conversion extended to the installation of a cooker, basic washing facilities, an Osokool storage cabinet, fitted cupboards, Calor gas and 6V DC electricity, in addition to comfortable sleeping, seating and dining facilities.

In order that purchase tax could be avoided, the vehicle had to be approved by ministry officials as living accommodation. To facilitate this, the vehicle was left at the premises of the local VW main dealer, Lisburne Garage Ltd of Torquay. Here it amassed considerable interest, with the result that it was placed in the garage's main showroom with a view to starting commercial production.

In essence, the Camper division of J. P. White (Sidmouth) Ltd came into being in July 1956, alongside Jack White's decision to use the county name as his brand. He was also responsible for inventing the term 'caravanette' and devising the name Caravette for the first model. Within six months of starting the business fifty-six vehicles had been sold through Lisburne Garages. Initially operating from Jack's garden shed, the business quickly graduated to his workshop at Sidford where all the beautiful solid oak units were made. Assembly also took place here if the completed Caravette was destined for a location in the south-west of England. However, in a move that illustrates the association between Volkswagen in Britain and Devon, orders destined for locations in other parts of the country were assembled at Volkswagen's own Dovercourt workshops based in Plaistow, London.

Despite a further move, there was still insufficient square footage of workshop space to cope with demand. Jack acquired the freehold interest in the Old Gas Works site in Sidmouth and constructed a purpose-built factory, which came to be known the length and breadth of the land as the Alexandria Works. Opened on 20 May 1960 and covering some 5 acres, plus fields and woodlands, not only was there sufficient room to produce the thousand or so vehicles ordered per year at the time, with a skilled workforce comprising of seventy-five local carpenters and craftsman, but also 'motor caravan accommodation' on land adjoining for customers new and old.

Unlike Westfalia, Devon tended to tweak their design annually and by the end of 1961 (for the 1962 season) were producing two options, the second being a new budget model named the Devonette, which joined the redesigned Caravette. Towards the end of 1965 this model was replaced by the Torvette, while both the new economy option and the Caravette were offered in two forms, 'standard' (for which read traditional bulkhead layouts), or 'spaceway', a walk-through option, which gained immediate popularity.

Sadly, Jack White wasn't on hand to see such developments as he died in November 1963, aged just fifty-one, the victim of a fatal heart-attack. His legacy lived on, albeit under new owners, throughout the era of the second-generation Transporter and beyond. Others, as has been said, gained a similar status in terms of official recognition for a time, but for many the name Devon is synonymous with the British Volkswagen Camper.

The Devon CARAVETTE

the ideal holiday home

MOTORISED CARAVAN ON
THE VOLKSWAGEN MICRO-BUS

Devon's brochures were inevitably not as lavish as those emerging from Wolfsburg. However, this example is a collector's piece. Dating from 1960, it features Jack White, founder of the Devon brand, his wife and children on the cover.

By the mid-sixties the covers of Devon brochures had been elevated to colour. This one dates from 1965. Even at the distance the Caravette is from the camera, it is easy to see that the conversion offered a comprehensive array of cabinets and accessories.

A hardworking Devon motor caravan
earns its holidays in the sun

The year is 1967 and Devon's brochure for the year is inspirational. The black and white image illustrates how the Camper can be used for the mundane things in life during the week, while the colour photograph captures the spirit of long summer holidays in the sun.

Epilogue – End of the Line and Survival in Brazil

While many will be aware that production of the first-generation Transporter ended in July 1967 at the Hanover factory to make way for a new model, far fewer will appreciate that a vehicle of its ilk continued in production at the Brazilian São Paulo factory for a further eight years, only coming to a halt in October 1975. Then and only then the Brazilian Kombi, as all models were known, gave way to a vehicle best described as an amalgamation of the German second-generation Transporter, at least as far as the front end went, and a variation on the Samba-style window arrangement of first-generation heritage.

In the region of 300,000 Brazilian Transporters, in the style of the first generation, were produced after the German range's demise, considerably more than in the nine years from 1957,

1975 and eight years after the demise of the German-built first-generation Transporter, here's the Fleetline. Manufactured in Brazil and assembled in South Africa, the budget-price Kombi, Pick-up and Delivery Van sold in South Africa alongside the more expensive second-generation models.

when Brazilian manufacture began, and the last weeks of 1966. Additionally, over 10,000 CKD kits were produced.

Curiously a percentage of the Brazilian CKD kits found their way to South Africa post-1967. Here, in addition to manufacturing the full range of second-generation Transporters, the Uitenhage factory assembled Brazilian Kombis to be sold at budget prices. In addition to a Delivery Van and a Pick-up, a Micro Bus with fifteen windows (similar in style to the German Samba, but without the roof skylights) was offered, each being sold under the brand name of Fleetline, a byword for value. South Africa's marketing department were strikingly honest regarding the origins of the vehicle that could 'move the load at old fashioned prices'.

> How can we afford to give you such a low, low price on our Fleetline vehicles? Well, first we import Transporter bodies from Brazil. Then we fit the latest rugged 1.6 litre engines that never quit. Once fully assembled, we're able to pass the saving on to you ... Inflation hasn't caught up with the Fleetline. And that means a lot of extra profit for you whether you're bussing people or carrying merchandise.

As Germany shipped both old dies and presses to Brazil, Transporters and kits manufactured and created at São Paulo carried many incongruous parts. For example, all Brazilian loading doors were essentially of the style fitted to pre-1955 German models. Early-style engine lids intermingled with much later style pull handles, later 14-inch wheels rubbed shoulders with early engine lids. The 1,500cc engine didn't become available as standard until 1966 and then remained to the end of production; rear lights were used in conjunction with pre-1963 corner windows and so on and so forth.

The last words, though, go to Brazil's marketing department, eager to sell the final examples of the old models – somehow, despite the passing of twenty-five years, the message hadn't really changed from Nordhoff's press conference to the first-generation Transporter finally bidding *despedida*.

> The Kombi is economic – on fuel, oil, parts and maintenance. You'll notice that it fits into your life and becomes an important factor in your work and enjoyment. During the week it works. It transports equipment, furniture, tools, machinery and almost anything else you need for your job. And on weekends it brings the whole family to the beach...

Bibliography

Copping, Richard, *Volkswagen Camper: Six Decades of Success* (Sparkford: Haynes Publishing, 2012)

Copping, Richard, *Volkswagen Transporter: A celebration of an automotive and cultural icon* (Sparkford: Haynes Publishing, 2011)

Copping, Richard, *Volkswagen Transporter: The First 60 Years* (Sparkford: Haynes Publishing, 2009)

Eccles, David, *VW Transporter and Microbus, Specification Guide, 1950–1967* (Ramsbury: The Crowood Press, 2002)

Eccles, David and Michael Steinke, *VW Bus and Pick-Up: Special Models* (Ramsbury: The Crowood Press, 2011)

Richter, Ralf, *Ivan Hirst: British Officer and Manager of Volkswagen's post-War Recovery* (Wolfsburg: Volkswagen AG group Communications, 2004)

Acknowledgements

The author and publisher would like to thank the following people/organisations for permission to use copyright material in this book: all archive pictures copyright Volkswagen Alktiengesellschaft. All archive pictures sourced from Volkswagen Alktiengesellschaft unless otherwise stated. Devon Camper material and pencil sketches by the late Robert Preis sourced from the library collated by Richard Copping.

With thanks to the keepers of the following vehicles for granting permission to photograph their VW Transporters: Paul Irvine – 1954 Double Door Delivery Van, 1952 15 Window Micro Bus De Luxe, 1967 Sundial Camper; Mike Johnstone – 1963 Moortown Motors Campahome; Ron Brown – 1960 15 Window Micro Bus De Luxe; Wayne Beattie – 1965 Westfalia SO44.

All modern-day photography copyright Richard A. Copping 2019.